JONAS KAUFMANN

JONAS KAUFMANN

In Conversation With

THOMAS VOIGT

WEIDENFELD & NICOLSON

First published in Great Britain in 2017
This paperback edition published in 2019 by Weidenfeld & Nicolson
an imprint of The Orion Publishing Group Ltd
Carmelite House, 50 Victoria Embankment
London EC4Y 0DZ

An Hachette UK Company

1 3 5 7 9 10 8 6 4 2

Copyright © 2015 by Henschel Verlag
in der Seemann Henschel GmbH & Co. KG, Leipzig, Germany

A CIP catalogue record for this book is
available from the British Library.

ISBN (paperback) 978 1 4746 0632 5
ISBN (ebook) 978 1 4746 0428 4

Typeset at The Spartan Press Ltd,
Lymington, Hants

Printed and bound by the CPI Group (UK) Ltd,
Croydon, CR0 4YY

www.orionbooks.co.uk

Contents

CONTENTS

'A singer entirely after my own heart'

Foreword by Plácido Domingo

I always enjoy hearing Jonas Kaufmann sing and invariably look forward to talking to him as a person, for he is not only a wonderful singer but also a highly intelligent artist who has spent a long time working on interpretative details of the roles in his repertory and examining questions of vocal technique. As such, he is a singer entirely after my own heart, fearlessly facing the challenges of performing German, Italian and French roles and working hard to ensure that every character is a credible and fully rounded individual.

I first saw him in Puccini's *La rondine* in London. It was his Covent Garden debut, and my wife and I were bowled over. We sensed straight away that here was an artist who could think for himself. Since then I have heard and seen him on many occasions. I was particularly impressed by his portrayal of Don José and will never forget the way in which he gradually evolved from the shy lad of the opening scenes to a man whom disappointment, despair and anger turn into a killer. He has the ability to hold an audience in the palm of his hand.

His decision not to limit himself to a particular repertory, or *Fach*, but to sing a wide range of roles is a very wise one, and I am convinced that he will be taking on Russian parts in the not-too-distant future, notably Hermann in *The Queen of Spades*. I regard this sort of variety as very healthy, because it means that the voice remains flexible and retains all its colours. And, as I know from my own experience, it is a good way of preserving your voice over a career lasting many decades.

Jonas told me that his voice teacher, Michael Rhodes, had been a pupil of the legendary Italian baritone Giuseppe De Luca (1876–1950), whose recordings include a number of duets with Caruso. My own roots do not go as far back as this, but I had the good fortune to hear many of the great singers of an earlier generation performing live and had the privilege of working with some of them. My first Edgardo, for example, was opposite the Lucia of Lily Pons, who was more than forty years older than me. In later years, too, I was able to learn a lot from older singers, sometimes by observing them closely but often by discussing technical and interpretative details with them. I am thinking here of Renata Tebaldi, Hans Hotter, Cesare Siepi, Robert Merrill, Birgit Nilsson, Regina Resnik, Ramón Vinay, Risë Stevens and many more.

For a number of years I have devoted a good deal of time and effort to encouraging talented young opera singers, either through my Operalia Competition or with my Young Artists Programs in Washington, Los Angeles and Valencia. Opera will remain a living art form only if older artists pass on their knowledge and experience to the younger generation. Jonas Kaufmann belongs to my sons' generation and for me he embodies the type of artist who, ideally, should be emerging all over the world. He seems to hold views similar to mine: he, too, is anxious to ensure that the torch is handed on. With his musicality, his vocal technique and his expressive powers – to say nothing of his matinée-idol good looks – he will be a model for many young people, which is why I am so pleased that he is now passing on his insights and his experiences to a new generation of singers.

It is a great honour for me to have the first word in this book. I wish Jonas Kaufmann all the happiness in the world and hope that he continues to be successful in all that he does.

'Dimmi quando, quando, quando...'

Introduction to the revised edition

~

The first major project on which Jonas Kaufmann and I worked together was a television documentary commissioned by the Stuttgart-based German broadcaster SWR, *Ein ganz normaler Held (A Completely Normal Hero)*. The producers, Wolfgang and Barbara Wunderlich, had planned to start filming in June 2008. Whenever I watch the film today, I immediately feel phantom limb pain since I had slipped a disc only a few days earlier and had difficulty walking. Indeed, the pain was so great that I could hardly sleep. My preferred option would have been to withdraw from the project completely. But I gritted my teeth and travelled to Zurich, where Jonas was rehearsing a new production of Bizet's *Carmen* with Vesselina Kasarova. Fortunately, the filming and the interviews all went well, and right from the outset the chemistry between Jonas and us seemed to work. We then accompanied him to the Schubertiade in Schwarzenberg, and by the time that we had recorded his lieder recital with Helmut Deutsch, I was glad that I had not cancelled.

Our next joint project was this book. Publishers had repeatedly approached Jonas about a biography, but his answer had always been the same: 'It's far too soon!' Now, however, there were various signs that someone was planning to write a book about him without his consent, with the result that he was forced to act very quickly. He called me and we agreed on a biography in the form of a series of interviews. Almost simultaneously the Leipzig-based publisher Seemann-Henschel announced that they were interested in publishing a book about Jonas, ideally to coincide with his Bayreuth debut in the summer of 2010. We did not have much time, as the manuscript would have to be submitted within a matter of only a few months. The final weeks were a race against the clock, but we managed to meet the deadline and were able to present our collaboration at a Bayreuth bookshop on the day after the first night of *Lohengrin*.

The event was so well attended that the shop's owner was forced to close the door on account of the crush. We were delighted, of course, and not even my minor faux pas at the end of the event could really cast a cloud over the occasion. At the first-night party the previous evening, Angela Merkel had asked Jonas if he was planning to sing any Russian roles: 'Hermann in *The Queen of Spades* would be a fantastic role for you!' 'I'd love to!' Jonas had replied, 'but I first need to learn Russian.' 'Well, let me know when you need my help,' the Chancellor had quipped in response. Someone then asked Jonas a similar question at the book-signing session the next day, prompting him to answer along similar lines: 'I first have to learn Russian!' At which point I blurted out: 'But you've already got a famous teacher!' Visibly embarrassed, Jonas reluctantly reported on his conversation with the Chancellor. The following day all of the newspapers carried the headline: 'Angela Merkel offers Jonas Kaufmann private Russian lessons.' We wrote to apologize for our indiscretion, saying that it had never been our intention to use the Chancellor's name to promote our cause.

The book was well received, both by the general public and by the press. Writing in the *Frankfurter Allgemeine Zeitung*, for example, the distinguished music journalist Eleonore Büning described it as 'the most compact, most sensible, most critical book on opera for a very long time'.

*

Throughout the months that followed I remained in constant contact with Jonas Kaufmann and his wife, Margarete. I performed various journalistic tasks for them and gradually took over as Jonas's press officer and dealt with the media. In practice this meant checking the accuracy of original quotations and approving the release of photographs and audio and video recordings, all of which was a source of considerable pleasure for me. The organizational aspect, conversely, was less appealing. In the case of an artist like Jonas Kaufmann, who even then was in demand all over the world, the constant requests for interviews, talk-show appearances, photoshoots and so on inevitably led to a backlog that in turn meant that people were kept waiting for a long time. There were many offers that Jonas would have been happy to accept, if only he had had the time. The number that he has sung most often is not Cavaradossi's 'E lucevan le stelle' but 'Dimmi quando, quando, quando' ('Tell me when').

'I have only one cake and everyone wants a slice of it,' he says on the subject of managing his time, no doubt aware that no one can satisfy all of the demands placed on them all of the time. Presumably he would like to have enough cakes to hand out to everyone. He finds it hard to say no, partly, no doubt, lest he seem arrogant. And on paper there are many events that are tempting: a Christmas show here, a gala dinner there, a red-carpet awards ceremony elsewhere. All too often, however, I have the impression that if I give these people an inch, they'll take a mile, and it is at this point that I feel the urge to protect Jonas. At moments like this I think that they should all give him some peace. It's all the more gratifying when, after endless toing and froing, everything passes off smoothly and at the end of the day one can be satisfied with the result.

A fun part of my work is the filming of his recording sessions. Mostly they involve Wolfgang Wunderlich (camera), his daughter Lena (stills) and Matthias Meinl (sound and second camera). We are a well-oiled team and have already made several television documentaries and video trailers with Jonas. The atmosphere has always been very relaxed. To date our joint projects include the Verdi album in Parma, the Puccini album in Rome, *Dolce Vita* in Palermo, *Das Lied von der Erde* in Vienna and what has so far been our most ambitious project, *Du bist die Welt für mich* (*You Mean the World to Me*). The atmosphere in the legendary Funkhaus Berlin in the Nalepastraße could hardly have been better. The songs by Franz Lehár, Emmerich Kálmán, Eduard Künneke, Paul Abraham and Robert Stolz are as popular as ever and everyone at the recording sessions was in a permanently good mood – there was always someone humming the tunes to themselves.

Jonas sang these songs with an enthusiasm and a natural flair that seemed to suggest he had sung nothing else for years. And yet it was an extremely demanding programme, ranging from Paul Abraham's 'Diwanpüppchen' ('Divan Dolly') to Eduard Künneke's 'Lied vom Leben des Schrenk' ('Song of Schrenk's Life'). The former requires a smoochy voice like that of Peter Alexander, whereas the latter demands a youthful and dramatic operatic tenor. It was written for Helge Rosvaenge, the hotspur among contemporary tenors and, vocally speaking, is no less demanding than the most difficult Verdi aria. Only days before the recording session, Jonas had in fact sung Don Alvaro in *La forza del destino* in Munich, performing the part with such bravura that no one on the recording team was seriously concerned about his ability to do justice to Künneke's song: 'If anyone can sing this today, it's Jonas!' After an astonishingly small number of takes the recording was in the can.

'A singer entirely after my own heart' is the heading that Plácido Domingo has given to his foreword to this volume. He speaks for many artists who have called on Jonas Kaufmann after a performance or a song recital. Marilyn Horne, Renata Scotto,

José Carreras, Sherrill Milnes, Barbara Cook, Emma Thompson, Georg Baselitz and Elizabeth Peyton are only a few of the professional singers, actors and painters who have felt the need to discuss their ideas with him.

Conversely, Jonas Kaufmann feels tremendous respect for those artists who have set new standards in their own profession, be they instrumentalists, conductors, singers, painters, architects, footballers or skiing champions. This explains why he refuses to live in a goldfish bowl but takes an interest in the most varied areas of public life. I hope that in the course of our conversations for this book we may be forgiven for merely touching on cinema, literature, football and cookery: an exhaustive account of all of these areas of interest would have taken us far beyond the scope of an interview-based biography.

More than seven years have passed since we launched the first edition of this book in Bayreuth, years of major successes but also a series of crises and low points, and I felt it was time for a revised and updated edition. I should like to take this opportunity to thank all of those people who have contributed to this volume: the busy guest authors who have generously placed their time and creative efforts at our disposal; and Jonas Kaufmann's colleagues and associates, all of whom have ensured that this portrait has so many different facets to it.

I am particularly grateful to Marion Tung, Alina Vlad and Karin Jacobs-Zander for their help in dealing with sensitive matters that arose in social media; to Dorothee Fleege for the conscientious way in which she has dealt with all requests from fans; to Alan Green, the late Bruce Zemsky and Stefan Pennartz for their support and advice; to the teams at Sony Music and Wunderlich Media; and, of course, to Jonas Kaufmann for placing his trust in me.

Thomas Voigt

The tenor as an object of desire

'A creature not of this world'

Berlioz proved strangely prescient when he asked in the sixth of his *Evenings with the Orchestra*, 'Don't you know that a tenor is a being apart [...]? He is a creature not of this world, he is a world in himself.' He was writing in the middle of the nineteenth century, long before the days of Caruso and the gramophone and at a time when sound films and television still lay in the distant future. Why are tenors a category unto themselves? Why are 'La donna è mobile' and 'Nessun dorma' popular hits in a way that is not the case with the arias of Rigoletto or Mimì? Why did Caruso pioneer the gramophone record and not Nellie Melba, who gave her name instead to a dish of peaches and ice cream? Why were Richard Tauber, Joseph Schmidt and Beniamino Gigli the vocal stars of the early talkies and not Maria Jeritza, who was the most attractive soprano of her age? Why were there 'The Three Tenors' and not 'The Three Sopranos'?

Tenors, it seems, inspire the masses to a far greater extent than other voice types. Why? The German philosopher Ernst Bloch described the tenor as the '*aurum potabile* of youth and erotic power'. He was referring in the first instance to the sound of the tenor voice, not to the singer's physical appearance: for a long time the principal reason why the tenor was an object of desire was the aural aspect, since from a purely visual standpoint, most tenors from Caruso to Gigli and Bergonzi tended to

9

correspond to the cliché of 'stocky and round'. Caruso was fond of poking fun at himself in his own self-caricatures and generally drew himself as a spherical body on short legs, with a large head and no neck. Lauritz Melchior, who remains unsurpassed as a heroic tenor, was described by the Met's general manager, Rudolf Bing, as a 'walking sofa'. Even in the early years of the sound film, there was just one genuine heart-throb of the silver screen, the Polish tenor Jan Kiepura.

Only in the wake of the Second World War was there a shift in perception and values. In 1951 it was not Jussi Björling – the 'Swedish Caruso' – who was chosen to play the lead in *The Great Caruso* but Mario Lanza, a singer who, vocally speaking, could not hold a candle to Björling. But he looked good on screen and was a decent actor. *The Great Caruso* marked the start of a new era: a God-given voice was no longer enough. From now on tenors also had to reflect our image of the romantic hero, at least in part. Of the new generation of tenors, some certainly cut a handsome figure: Mario Del Monaco, for example, and Giuseppe di Stefano. Rudolf Schock played a trapeze artist in the 1954 Austrian film *König der Manege* (*King of the Circus Ring*) and was every bit as dashing as he was as Bacchus alongside the Ariadne of the exceptionally beautiful Lisa Della Casa. By the end of the decade North America had produced two muscular heavyweights in the form of Jon Vickers and Jess Thomas as well as a number of singing actors like James King, who had the physique of a trained sportsman.

The ideal of the Latin lover was embodied at the time by Franco Corelli. Over six feet two inches tall, he looked like a Hollywood star and had a magnificent voice to match, with top notes to die for. As a result, listeners were inclined to forgive him for making Meyerbeer's Raoul and Massenet's Werther sound like Puccini's Cavaradossi. He suffered from acute stage fright, and there were times when he quite literally had to be pushed out onto the stage. But then he would sing like a god.

Little needs to be said about the impact of The Three Tenors, who took their operatic hits to the football stadiums of the world. Their first concert at the World Championships in Rome in 1990 was an unparalleled marketing coup that ushered in a new era and heralded the advent of the tenor as a multimedia megastar. Each, in his own way, reflected the concept of the tenor as the embodiment of a uniquely 'erotic power'. Listeners who are familiar with Pavarotti only from his overweight final years should take a look at photographs and videos from the early 1970s to understand why an American women's magazine could describe the baker's son from Modena as one of the 'sexiest men of the year'. And anyone who ever saw Plácido Domingo and José Carreras besieged by their armies of fans will be aware of the power that can be exerted by such an erotic force, turning mature women into screaming groupies.

The Three Tenors were followed by three other singers who were hailed as their successors: José Cura, Roberto Alagna and Rolando Villazón. A mere glance at reports of these three singers reveals that audiences now react with their eyes to a far greater extent than was the case only twenty or thirty years ago. Cura's appearance as a Latin lover and Villazón's total commitment as an actor have resulted in more detailed and more subtly differentiated accounts of their stage performances than of their vocal achievements.

'A sex symbol in the service of opera'

It was just when Villazón was suffering from a vocal crisis of his own that a new 'heir apparent' emerged on the scene in January 2008 in the person of Jonas Kaufmann. After his Met debut in 2006 he had already been invited to appear at every other leading opera house, but it was his first solo album, *Romantic Arias*, that really seemed to seal his status as a world-class tenor made in Germany. When the CD was released, every television channel carried reports on performances of *La traviata* in London with Anna Netrebko and Kaufmann: the beautiful Russian and the attractive German. It was rumoured, of course, that Kaufmann was to be marketed as Netrebko's new partner. It was an obvious idea since both were under contract with Universal, two of whose labels, Deutsche Grammophon and Decca, could look back on a long tradition in the classical music industry. But the fact of the matter is that the recording contract had been signed long before there was any talk of Villazón's vocal crisis or of a production of *La traviata* with Netrebko and Kaufmann.

The series of photographs that were taken for Kaufmann's first solo album for Decca certainly contributed to the shift of focus from ears to eyes: 'The handsomest man in opera' (*Bild*), 'The handsomest tenor in the world' (*Bild*), 'The Latin lover of the Leopoldstraße' (*Die Zeit online* – a reference to one of Munich's main thoroughfares), 'As sexy as Brad' (*stern*), 'The new Adonis among male divas' (*stern.de*) – and so it went on in all of the media. The headline in *Gramophone* magazine seemed positively understated by contrast: 'Stage animal'. But it hit the nail on the head. Unsurprisingly, Kaufmann soon grew tired of people concentrating on his physical appearance and he signalled that being a sex symbol was 'of only secondary importance'. Over the years he has come to adopt a more relaxed approach to this issue, and when he posed for the weekend supplement, *Io Donna*, of the Italian daily *Corriere della sera* in the spring of 2014, the question could hardly be avoided, prompting him to answer: 'If this way I can get people to come to the opera who would otherwise not set foot in an opera house, then that's all right by me.' In saying this, he opened the way for the supplement's headline: 'Sex symbol al servizio della lirica' ('A sex symbol in the service of opera').

Typecasting

A singer must have ambivalent feelings about being described as handsome and sexy. No one who sings wants to be judged by their appearance alone. How do you deal with such judgements?

It took me a while to break free from this image and to be taken seriously by certain people. True, it certainly can't be a matter of indifference to a singer in the age of DVDs, websites and YouTube clips what he looks like and whether he is at all credible in the role that he is performing. And it can't harm you, of course, if it says in the paper that you're 'handsome and sexy'. But if it is only about superficialities and has nothing to do with my roles, then I'd prefer not to read it at all. And one thing should be absolutely clear: it may be easier to get to the top if you look good, but there is no doubt that you'll be able to remain at the top only if you have the requisite vocal quality.

Except that vocal qualities on their own have been insufficient for some time now.

That's true, and that's a good thing. Nor is it just about acting. Opera, after all, is music plus theatre, but singers shouldn't have to look like dancers or models: our profession needs completely different types of people. And what matters in a particular role isn't good looks but, above all, credibility. That's why I prefer roles that have more character to them, more sharp edges than the typical Latin-lover parts in the tenor repertory: characters like Don Carlo, Don José and Dick Johnson in Puccini's *La fanciulla del West*.

Typecasting has often produced some weird results. At what point do you reach your pain threshold?

When first-class singers are replaced by mediocre ones because they don't look so great or are less telegenic. Or if a gifted singer is from the outset denied a decent career because she doesn't live up to today's expectations. During my time as a student there was a soprano who had a wonderful voice, but she was told at college: 'You'll never make it because you're far too fat, fatter than most tenors. So you can forget it.' That's insane. Typecasting is ultimately the expression of a lack of imagination – not just on the part of theatre managers but also on that of journalists and audiences. What's so wonderful about opera is that we enter a foreign world that springs from our imagination and from the power of the music. It's not a reality show but an enchanted world. If, in opera, you try to show people what they can already see in their everyday lives, there may be a certain appeal to this, but it robs opera of all its magic, it disempowers the music and deprives the performers of their power of conviction.

So it wouldn't disturb you to see a size-eighteen Salome?

If she has a great voice, sings the role wonderfully well and exudes a sense of eroticism, then it doesn't matter to me at all whether she has the physique for the Dance of the Seven Veils. And if she herself is comfortable with her own body, then the aura that she radiates will be the right one. This inner balance is essential for every singer. But if she herself feels that she has a weight problem, then she should consider how best to deal with it.

The general dislike of fat sopranos ('It ain't over 'til the fat lady sings') persuaded Deborah Voigt to undergo gastric-bypass surgery to reduce the size of her stomach and allow her to lose weight. Even relatively slim singers have said that they need tremendous self-discipline to stay in shape. Why is this? After all, singing is a high-performance sport and a singer's calorie intake needs to be correspondingly high.

I think it has a lot to do with questions of lifestyle. You've given a performance and your adrenalin level is raised to goodness knows what. You're still feeling pumped up, you're hungry and you seek out the company of others. And so you go for a meal after the performance. By then it's often after midnight. Or you empty the minibar in your hotel room. When you're alone on tour, you often stuff yourself out of sheer frustration. I've frequently caught myself doing just that. But whether you are alone or in good company, the temptation to eat too much or too late or both is everywhere, especially in Italy.

What do you do when you realize that you've gained weight?

I swim, I play tennis. But I've never trained in a gym. I may do so if it becomes necessary – but not strength training and certainly not anabolic steroids, which would have an immediate and adverse effect on my voice, to say nothing of all the other side effects.

Being a singer and having a six-pack are said to be mutually exclusive. Why's that?

Because singers have to remain as elastic and flexible as possible in their diaphragm area. Exaggeratedly powerful stomach muscles tend to get in the way of your breathing, which needs to be measured and to flow freely. In your throat area, too, you need to remain relaxed. The more tense you are and the more rigid the vocal cords become, the less they can vibrate. I've yet to meet a tenor who has a well-toned body and a large and healthy voice.

In terms of your physique, one might think you were a baritone, not a tenor.

That's exactly what a doctor once said to me: 'You have the physiognomy of a baritone.' Tenors are typically short, round, rather stocky and have a short neck. Well, who knows, perhaps I'm a baritone with an extended top. But as long as I can sing tenor roles, that's fine by me.

Exhibitionism and eroticism

An opera singer's profession requires on the one hand the ability to be part of a team, as in the chamber music ensembles in operas like Così fan tutte, Falstaff *and* Ariadne auf Naxos, *and on the other hand it requires unbridled egoism and exhibitionism. Can these qualities be reconciled within a single person?*

Absolutely. You just need to know when it's the turn of the 'chamber musician' and when it's that of the 'stage animal' hogging the footlights. In the final trio from *Der Rosenkavalier*, for instance, I'd find it grotesque if all three women were to try to prove which one of them had the biggest voice. Here it is art that matters most, and the more the three of them take account of one another, the more beautiful the trio sounds. But then there are passages where the audience expects this extra dash of exhibitionism, for example at the cries of 'Vittoria! Vittoria!' in *Tosca*. It now amuses me to give people what they want and I am no longer as reserved as I was in my first *Tosca* in Vienna. Afterwards Christa Ludwig came to see me in my dressing room and said something along the lines of 'You sing all of this in such a refined and cultivated tone, but as Cavaradossi you sometimes have to hog the footlights as Corelli used to do.' She's right. We Central Europeans tend to be relatively backward in putting ourselves forward. It's not easy for us to let rip in the uninhibited way that most Italian and Spanish singers do. But this is precisely what audiences want: they demand this extra thrill, this large-scale emotion that can be felt on an almost physical level. This is an essential part of the fascination of opera, and whenever I find myself sitting in the audience, this is exactly what I too demand.

Why is it that it's tenors who are regarded as the embodiment of an 'erotic power', even though baritones and basses sound more manly when judged by current standards?
That would be an interesting topic for further discussion, because a high C takes tenors into a female singer's vocal range. But perhaps this is exactly what many listeners find so exciting.

And what about your effect on your stage partners? What do you do if, in a love scene, a female colleague blurs the boundaries between stage and private life?
Initially I pretend not to notice, since most of the time your work together is limited to only a few weeks. It's not as if you're sitting in the same office for twenty years. But if the signals continue, you need to talk to each other in order to resolve the situation. This has already happened to me; it's to be expected in our line of work as we find ourselves in the very special situation of always having to pretend.

'The new king of tenors'

How do you feel about superlatives such as 'the new king of tenors'?
Of course, I feel flattered and think: 'Well, all that hard work has paid off!' But superlatives are as double-edged as exaggerated compliments about my appearance. After all, what's the point of deciding which artists are 'the best', 'the greatest'? Our profession is interesting not least because we can offer such a

huge range of interpretative possibilities. Why should we try to establish which is the 'best' recording of a symphony or an opera when we can enjoy the most disparate readings of it? I'd never want to forgo this variety, and it would be good if we had more than just a 'dream cast' for certain pieces.

Some years ago I asked a well-known journalist to take part in a survey for Opernwelt's *yearbook. 'I'm honoured,' he replied, 'but I don't like surveys designed to determine who is the "most pregnant" or "most amputated"'.*

Even so, *Opernwelt* has a category for 'Singer of the Year', not for the 'Best Singer'. There's a difference. On principle, however, superlatives are problematic even for the recipient, because they invite contradiction. The more often someone is placed on a pedestal, the more some people enjoy casting them down. And the higher the pedestal, the greater the fall. That's true not only of football but of our own profession, too. It seems to be an inevitable part of playing in the top league. You're never safe.

But how safe can anyone be in such an exposed position? Artists who have made it to the top tend to be the ones most plagued by self-doubt. This seems almost to be a general rule – it's effectively the price of success.

I regard self-doubt as an important corrective and as a necessary counterweight to the cast-iron sense of self-confidence that a singer obviously needs to have – otherwise you would never set foot on a stage. But it should never turn into complacency. You should never think: 'It doesn't matter what I do, people will still like me!' Healthy doubts, coupled with self-reflection, are absolutely essential for every developing artist. A singer who only ever thinks that he's great will never take another step forward.

The first twenty-five years

Anyone who was born in Munich – a city known to Italians as 'Monaco di Baviera' – and who speaks Italian as well as you do and who looks to be from the Mediterranean must always be asked the same question.

Do I have Italian ancestry? We've traced our family tree as far back as we can go but so far we've not been able to discover anything. Even so, it's a well-documented fact that in the wake of the persecution of the Jews in the Middle Ages a number of Italian artisans came to Thuringia, which is where my ancestors settled. Almost everyone on my mother's side looks Mediterranean, and so we assume that one of these immigrants was among our ancestors.

Where did your parents grow up?

They both grew up in Thuringia and both of them fled from the German Democratic Republic in the 1950s. But they didn't get to know each other until they were both living in the West. It was at a dance in Munich in 1956. There's no doubt that the shared experience of their East German past helped to bring them together. They got married in 1958. My sister, Katrin, was born in 1964; I followed in 1969. I grew up in Munich, in Bogenhausen, a housing development that had only just been built as part of a social housing programme. The buildings there tend to be plain and uniform with small windows, but between the houses there are huge areas of grass, so it was a natural paradise for children.

Were your parents professional musicians?
No, my mother had trained as a kindergarten teacher, but as a Protestant in Catholic Bavaria she was unable to teach and so she worked for a building contractor until the birth of my sister. My father – he died following an operation in 1994 – worked for an insurance company. His job involved a lot of detailed analysis and he had to write reports on major accidents running to several pages, but he could hardly have been less like your typical insurance broker. He was very fond of people and took an interest in all things cultural. His great love was classical music. Whenever he could, he listened to the classical music station of Bavarian Radio and went to concerts. And he had a large collection of records.

Wagner and Puccini

How did you come to music?
Initially through my paternal grandfather, Fritz, playing the piano. He lived in the same building, two floors above us, but his flat was too small for a piano. We had one, however, and so he would come down to our flat every morning and play for hours at a time. He was a real Wagnerian and owned vocal scores of all the Wagner operas. Whenever he played from them, he would sing all the parts, from Hagen to Brünnhilde. To that extent Wagner was a part of my upbringing. I grew up with this music and found it fascinating to leaf through my grandfather's scores. They were beautifully designed editions with wonderful illustrations of the sets from old productions and tables listing the leitmotifs. So I got to know the magic of Wagner's music in what I'd describe as a playful way.

And did your grandfather inspire you to play the piano yourself?
I think that at that time my pleasure in listening to him was greater than any urge to play myself. That came only after my sister had already been having piano lessons for several years. I didn't want to be left out, a feeling often found among siblings. My mother regularly got on to us about it and made us practise at home – much to the dismay of our neighbours. But it was never much fun, so my piano playing didn't get very far. I envy singers who can accompany themselves. Unfortunately, I can't. Singing was much more fun, especially the traditional carols in the Christmas market on the Marienplatz in Munich. It was a great privilege to be allowed to perform on these occasions. Children's choirs from the whole of Bavaria fought for the chance to do so, but our choir was one of the select few to be chosen, not least as a result of the work of our enterprising choirmaster. I can still see us standing on the Town Hall balcony and singing carols with great fervour, our noses turned bright red by the cold. Down below us, among the decorated stands and the big Christmas tree, were our parents, visibly proud.

You also listened to records together.
It was a regular ritual at home, mostly on Sundays. While Catholics attended church, we listened to classical music. My sister and I would then sit on the brown leather sofa in our living room and were allowed to choose a record. We weren't permitted to touch the expensive vinyl discs and someone else always had to turn them over. Later we acquired a cassette player, which meant that we could finally listen to a whole symphony without a break and also record music from the radio. But we also had some great children's records of classical music such as *Piccolo, Sax & Co*. These provided us with an introduction to the different instruments, and while listening to them we imagined ourselves on a musical tour of the world.

How old were you when you first went to the opera?

Six or seven. It was a Sunday-afternoon family performance of Puccini's *Madama Butterfly* at the Bavarian State Opera. For me it was the classic formative experience. Even today I can still feel the side parting in my well-brushed hair and can still remember my white shirt and traditional Bavarian costume. I sat next to my sister in the front row, right in the middle, directly behind the conductor. It was tremendous. Everything was beautiful and exciting. The vast auditorium, the red velvet upholstery on the seats, the sets, the costumes, the music and then the applause. And suddenly the woman who had just stabbed herself was standing there in front of the curtain and had come back to life! I simply couldn't make sense of it. For me opera was so truthful, so genuine and serious. That's how I felt at the time, and to a certain extent it has remained so ever since. My sister, five years older, saw the performance through very different eyes: 'I'm amazed you thought it so great! The soprano perspired so much that her make-up started to run. I couldn't stop staring and couldn't think of anything else.' That's how much our perceptions differed.

My father was very supportive of my passion for opera. The next performance I saw at the Nationaltheater was *Eugene Onegin*, this time an evening performance, so I got home correspondingly late. My father wrote a letter that I handed to my teacher the following morning and which said something along the lines of: 'Jonas was at the opera yesterday, it was a great experience for him, but since he didn't get home until 11.00, he'll no doubt be a bit dozy today. I hope you won't mind.'

Bella Italia

Among the popular songs associated with the years of Germany's economic miracle were some that invited their listeners to travel south to Italy and to the Mediterranean. In fact, for many German families Italy was the Promised Land at that time.

My family had been in love with Italy long before the Germans started descending on the country in waves and developed a love of all things Italian. If I remember correctly, it was my grandfather who set the ball rolling. He had spent much of the war in Turin and always spoke enthusiastically about his time there, saying that we absolutely had to go there ourselves. In the event it wasn't Turin that we visited but the Adriatic – for the first few years it was always the same place and the same apartment. Initially the journey was relatively arduous as there was a motorway for only a few sections of the way, so it took a good day's driving to get there. At some point my father grew tired of always seeing the same sights. He had taught himself to speak good Italian, and Goethe's longing for Italy was in his blood. He also liked to avoid the beaten track, so he planned a mixture of a beach holiday and visits to places of cultural interest. He prepared it in minute detail using travel guides and books on art, so we were able to glean some wonderful impressions in a relatively short space of time. During this period my dream was to become an archaeologist. I was so drawn to archaeological digs that it was impossible to drag me away. I can still remember how annoyed my family would get each time I spent hours rummaging in the sand in the hope of unearthing a particularly spectacular find. But with hindsight I have to say that it is to these visits to places of cultural interest that I ultimately owe my fondness for the Italian language. We got to know not only the country but also the people, forging friendships that have lasted for many years. Eventually my sister no longer wanted her little brother following her every step and preferred to meet young men, so at that point I was forced to learn Italian – and for that I'm eternally grateful. Learning the language at an early stage among Italians is undoubtedly one of the reasons why I'm now accepted as a Puccini and Verdi singer in Italy. To that extent our holidays in Italy were the basis of my *italianità*.

Which also reveals itself in your love of making coffee. The world has lost a barista in you.

(*laughing*) Coffee and sweet things are among my great passions. The smell of freshly ground beans, the gentle hum of the machine, the first espresso have become an indispensable ritual; there's no other way that I want to start the day. And, as with all great passions, you immerse yourself in it more and more with the passing years as you want to know how it works. What does it mean when you replace a fully automatic coffee machine with a lever espresso machine? And before you buy such a machine, you naturally do your homework and find out how to make the best coffee, where you can buy the best coffee beans and so on. At some point you are so spoilt that you rarely enjoy coffee outside Italy, unless you've made it yourself or you meet people who have immersed themselves as deeply in the subject as you have. This way a passion eventually turns into an obsession. When we recorded the album of Italian songs in Palermo, I discovered a wonderful old roasting house, and ever since then I've got them to send me regular shipments of coffee and look forward to it every morning with childlike delight. If the espresso runs out of the machine like thick chocolate, I feel a sense of happiness that I miss every time I find myself standing at the hotel buffet and don't have my own machine and my own coffee beans.

My fondness for sweet things goes hand in hand with this. I was very spoilt at home. For us, coffee and cakes were simply a part of an enjoyable weekend, and my mother was a wonderful cook. Unfortunately I rarely have time for this myself, so I stick to what's on offer in good cafés. On this point, too, Italy is unbeatable, although Austrian baking isn't to be sneezed at.

Among my all-time favourites are the Kardinalsschnitten (cardinal slices) in the Café Schatz in Salzburg.

Anyone who gets out and about as much as you and who enjoys good food as you do generally knows where to find the best pizza, the best carbonara and so on.
I know certain places that I always return to, that's true. But I'm also grateful for tips. When we recorded *Aida* in Rome, Mauro Bucarelli of the Accademia di Santa Cecilia gave me the address of a pizzeria around twenty minutes by taxi from the city centre. He told us to go there and he'd catch us up later. We arrived and suspected he was having a joke at our expense. We looked at each other and thought that any moment he would emerge laughing from behind a wall. The whole area looked shady, and the restaurant itself didn't exactly seem inviting, but the pizzas were the best that I'd eaten in years.

The worst possible troublemaker

Back to your childhood. What were you like at school?
Today a psychologist would probably speak of a classic attention deficit disorder. I was hyperactive, I soon got bored, I was rebellious and cheeky and was always fooling around and getting caught up in pranks. My parents knew intuitively that there is only one thing you can do in such cases: avoid every kind of boredom and ensure that the child is constantly challenged. And so they enrolled me at a traditional grammar school near the Isar, where the focus was on the humanities. Latin and Ancient Greek were still taught there, and the spirit of 1968 had yet to invade its hallowed precincts. In spite of this, the school had somehow contrived to accept girls. Initially, I was in a class consisting entirely of thirty-three boys, including a number of rebels and hooligans, and we soon formed a

clique of our own. Unfortunately, this meant that my parents' strategy – 'The more effort he has to make, the less trouble he'll be' – was overtaken by events. We were forever hatching some new scheme or other, and our teachers really had their hands full with us. The situation eventually became so bad that at a staff meeting it was decided to exclude the worst troublemaker from the class. That was me. The headmaster himself assumed responsibility for implementing this disciplinary measure, and in the spring of 1983 I had to leave the clique. But every cloud has its silver lining, and I was transferred to a co-educational class – with girls!

By now you were thirteen or fourteen. What had happened in the meantime to your passion for opera?
It had abated somewhat or, rather, it had taken second place to other interests. When we were at home, my sister and I now tended to listen to current pop and rock songs in the charts, which we recorded on our little cassette player. In my room I had a corner devoted to Bayern Munich, including a poster signed by Franz Beckenbauer and Paul Breitner, not to mention the obligatory Bayern scarf elegantly draped across the wall. I'm still a Bayern fan today.

What part did music lessons play at your school?
An important one and, in my own case, one that shaped my whole life. With the passage of time the younger teachers at the school had succeeded in creating a more relaxed atmosphere, and one of them, Bernd Schuch, was a music teacher and choir-master who was as committed as he was ambitious. There was a choir for the younger pupils who were still learning to sing and a chamber choir for more advanced singers. Even as a child I'd found choral singing great fun, so I really enjoyed being in the school choir. I can't remember ever going there reluctantly. At least two hours a week were set aside for the rehearsals,

and prior to a concert we would work on the programme up to three times a week. I thought it was brilliant. But when, at a rehearsal, Schuch asked me to sing the tenor solos at our Christmas concert, I was initially unhappy as I felt embarrassed about singing in front of my school friends and was inhibited when it came to performing – which was certainly not the case with talking. On one occasion Schuch threw me out for talking during the rehearsals. Out of sheer defiance I didn't return for six months. But I then turned a corner, not just in music but also with girls. What annoyed me during this period was the fact that we only ever sang classical music in the choir, even though we kept asking to sing other kinds of music.

What sort of music did you listen to in private at the time?
Peter Gabriel, Genesis, Dire Straits, AC/DC – and the Alan Parsons Project! They were all in the charts for weeks on end. Also popular at this time was the title song from *La Boum* (*The Party*), a cult film among teenagers in the years around 1980. And we took our first tentative steps in the direction of cheek-to-cheek dancing to the sound of *Dreams Are My Reality*.

In the extra chorus at the Theater am Gärtnerplatz

You were seventeen when you made your operatic debut as a member of the chorus at Munich's Theater am Gärtnerplatz. How did that come about?
Through a newspaper ad. They wanted to boost their extra chorus. I went to the auditions and became the youngest member of the choir, which at that time comprised around twenty singers. Since the theatre gave regular performances of operas, operettas and musicals with large choruses, we always had something to do – which additionally provided me with

some welcome extra pocket money. But the decisive factor was that for the first time I was on the opposite side of the footlights. This feeling of being up there right next to the soloists is something I'll never forget. I could feel them breathing, could experience at first hand the power and the affecting tenderness of their performances – and for the first time I myself was a part of the action. So I not only learnt to love opera, but I also practised for my later profession while I was still at school – even though I didn't know it at the time.

A fellow member of the chorus, who regularly appeared onstage with you at that time, has described you as a 'cheeky monkey'.
I won't have been much different from what I was like at school: happy, cheeky, carefree, impertinent, a bit rebellious and anarchical. With this mixture people soon make friends, but they also, unintentionally, make enemies – by questioning a director's instructions in front of the entire cast, for example.

How were you able to reconcile this side job with your final years at school?
Very easily. Of course, I was often very tired after a performance and the subsequent socializing, but even here I was lucky. For the first time in the history of our school, a whole series of fortunate circumstances meant that music was now an advanced course for pupils in their last two years at school. I'd originally intended to choose maths and physics as my advanced courses, but then I discovered that the music course still needed one person to make up the required numbers. I had no desire to practise the piano for several hours a day as part of the instrumental part of the course, and so the school looked for a way out of this impasse and sent me to audition at the College of Music. Here I received the Ministry's special authorization: instead of playing the piano I could sing as part of my schoolleaving exam – on condition that I received regular singing

28

lessons from a professional. And so I had classes twice a week with Christof Schuppler at the College of Music.

Once the principal troublemaker, now some exotic creature who sang as part of his school-leaving exam – didn't this turn you into an outsider?
No, it was more a question of being thrust into the limelight because of my singing. When the class was in Rome, for example, we lads had met a group of Italian girls and tried to make some sort of contact with them, but they gave us the cold shoulder. Of course, this merely spurred us on: we followed them and waited outside the building that they'd entered in order to see what would happen. After a few minutes a light went on in one of the upstairs rooms and one of the girls came out onto the balcony to see if we'd followed them. My classmates immediately started to badger me: 'Listen, you can sing, do something, sing some Italian song.' Which I did, at the top of my voice. I can't bear to think what it must have sounded like. True, I'd had singing lessons, but I'm sure it can't have been great. I also had to contend with the noise from the street, so that volume was by no means a negligible factor. In spite of all this, it had its effect, and it was fascinating to see the cars slowing down in the busy street and their occupants winding down their windows. Even in Rome, it's not an everyday sight for someone to sing in the street. But it was of no use. The girls listened for a while and then they closed the windows, and that was that.

Far more successful was your first appearance in Africa, in Malawi in 1987.
It was a cultural exchange programme supported by the Bavarian Chancellery as well as by various foreign aid organizations such as Médecin sans Frontières. We were a group of students, mostly studying music, and we'd rehearsed a number of pieces such as *Carmina Burana* and *Carnival of the Animals*.

After a week as exchange students in a kind of elite school we toured the country and were guests of German families living in the country's capital, Lilongwe. A highlight of the tour was our reception by Malawi's President, Hastings Banda. He sat in a wheelchair on the balcony of his house. It was quite a comical situation, not least when a couple of men turned up with microphones. We were told they were setting up a temporary radio station, which is how we learnt that our concert was to be broadcast on the radio. I belted out a couple of arias, including 'La donna è mobile'. That was more or less my radio debut as a soloist.

Can you remember what you sang for your school-leaving exam?
I think it was the first six songs from *Winterreise*.

Maths or music?

Maths or music – that was the big question after you'd sat your school-leaving exam. You decided to study maths and enrolled in a course of study.
I was following my parents' advice. It was intended to be something solid, something where I could be certain of finding a job, like my father, who had a decent income and who was able to take care of his family. I too wanted a family, and it was also clear to me that professional singing is quite a risk: you're especially dependent on your health, and even a minor cold can leave you unable to work. Also, I already knew some chorus singers who would have liked to become soloists but for whom this hadn't worked out. I had all of this at the back of my mind when I decided to study maths. I persevered for a couple of terms, but throughout this time I felt increasingly certain that I wasn't born to be a theorist or to do a desk job. So I finally decided to take the entrance exam for the College of Music and

to study singing – I was accepted at the first attempt. After that it took a lot of courage to abandon the comfortable security of a maths degree.

How did your parents react?
They were worried, of course, and unsure whether I'd get far enough to survive as a singer – with hindsight I think that this was better than them saying, 'Yes, of course, go for it, you're gifted, something is bound to come of it!' To fail after being encouraged in this way is far worse than gradually overcoming your own doubts and worries.

Fortunately the pressure that I put myself under soon vanished, and when I look back on this period now, I have to say that my time as a student was totally carefree. We only had one or two voice lessons a week. My advanced course in music from my time at school meant that I was well up on the history and theory of music, so the time and effort that I had to put into studying was kept within limits, and the Italian classes were almost unnecessary because, thanks to our holidays in Italy, I could already speak the language fluently. But it was the acting class where I felt most comfortable: it was a new little world that fascinated me a lot. All in all, there was still lots of time for the good things in life. We hung around in cafés and beer gardens and had a great deal of fun. In the eyes of Helmut Deutsch, who was my teacher for lieder singing, I was a 'carefree, happy-go-lucky person who goes to no unnecessary lengths and knows how to enjoy life'.

Gigs and bit parts

But you need money to enjoy yourself. How did you get by at that time?
There were two sources of income available to me. One consisted of occasional jobs, or gigs, while the other was BMW,

where I worked as a VIP chauffeur for a number of years. I already had the obligatory dark suit in my wardrobe as I'd bought one for my concert appearances, so I just had to sacrifice part of my magnificent mane. BMW paid well and I was able to afford my own car, not a BMW, it's true, but my grandfather's bright-green VW Golf. Mobility is practically a precondition for gigs, which are often held in places barely accessible by public transport. But my own transport also offered plenty of other opportunities. Even then I rarely stayed in one place for any length of time but was always on the go. The boot of the car contained everything I needed for trips: a little camping table, two deckchairs and a set of picnic utensils.

How did things progress at the Theater am Gärtnerplatz? How long were you in the extra chorus? And when did you get your first bit parts with one or two lines to sing?

I spent three or four years in the extra chorus at the Gärtnerplatz. I sang my first bit parts in the Bavarian provinces, mostly in productions by a privately run touring company that performed in the ballrooms in country hotels from Miesbach to Weilheim. In performances of *Sleeping Beauty*, for example, I contributed the two critical words 'Look there!' Later I even made it to the Bavarian State Opera with some of these bit parts and was able to read my name at the very bottom of the cast list as 'Messenger' or the like. But I found it inspiring to work on some great projects such as the world premiere of Michèle Reverdy's *Le précepteur* as part of the Munich Biennale, an international festival for new works of music theatre that was founded by Hans Werner Henze in 1988. One of the highlights of my bit-part repertory was the world premiere of Krzysztof Penderecki's avant-garde opera *Ubu Rex*. The production was by August Everding and took place at the Bavarian State Opera. I had the privilege of playing two parts, a Polish peasant and a Russian soldier, and of appearing onstage alongside such famous singers as Robert Tear and Doris Soffel. That was my actual debut at the State Opera, on Saturday, 6 July 1991.

Four days before your twenty-second birthday. In the 1950s it was by no means unusual for such young singers to appear on international stages, but by your generation it was already the exception: people say that German music colleges had been ivory towers, and only those singers who, like you, had the occasional experience of daily life in an opera house really knew what it was like to be a singer let loose in the wild.

With hindsight I can confirm that. At the time I simply used the opportunity to earn some money and gain practical experience with these bit parts. My time at college was less a chance to prepare for the day-to-day life of a singer than a way of acquiring a comprehensive basic training: learning the repertory, studying roles and gaining an understanding of ensemble work, of dancing and fencing, acting and lieder singing. And, of course, we rehearsed not just individual arias and ensembles but also entire pieces: Britten's *A Midsummer Night's Dream*, Strauss's *Ariadne auf Naxos* and Ravel's *L'heure espagnole*, for example. There were always public performances at the end of term. In other words, the course was by no means lacking in practical experience, but we were very cosseted on the grounds that we would all too soon get to know the harsher aspects of life in the theatre.

How stressful were the gondola rides in Regensburg during the 1993–4 season? After all, you were still a student at that time. Having to sing thirty-six performances of Eine Nacht in Venedig (A Night in Venice) *must have been like being thrown in at the deep end.*

It wasn't really the deep end, and in any case I already knew how to swim. But I was still a bit naïve at that time. And Caramello is undoubtedly a demanding role that requires an experienced tenor and a good actor. He sings the 'Gondola Song', a world-famous number that I knew from recordings by Rudolf Schock and others. He's also in most of the ensembles. But they trusted me, I trusted myself, and the college authorities gave me their blessing. It was enormous fun: it's wonderful music, especially in the Korngold version, and whenever I think of it, I'm overwhelmed by the desire to work on another operetta production.

Lessons with three vocal legends: James King, Josef Metternich and Hans Hotter

'Jonas Kaufmann is a dynamic and ebullient Tamino and will one day surely sing Florestan,' we read in a review of a student production of Die Zauberflöte *under Colin Davis at the Prinzregententheater in June 1994. That's quite an accolade for a beginner.*

It certainly pleased me at the time, even though I was perfectly clear in my own mind that Florestan was still a very long way off. All the greater was my pleasure when, shortly afterwards, I was accepted for a place at August Everding's vocal academy in Munich, specifically in the class given by James King, who had made operatic history in *jugendlich-dramatisch* roles such as Florestan, Lohengrin, Parsifal and Siegmund. He was then around seventy, a super-friendly person but one who sang completely intuitively, certainly not a technician who thought long and hard about what he did. And so he brought with him one of his own teachers from the Juilliard School, who tried to wean me off the habit of applying too much pressure while singing. On one occasion he laid me backwards over the piano stool like a bow, so that my stomach was abnormally stretched. He then made me sing, because in this position the diaphragm can't contract. I also attended a masterclass given by Josef Metternich, with whom I'd already been having private lessons for some time, even though this was forbidden by the college. I tried out everything he showed me, throwing myself into it with great enthusiasm and in the process quickly becoming hoarse. I understood what I needed to do to improve but my body wasn't yet able to put it into practice. Even so, the lessons that I had with him were great fun, he was a real character and I liked him a lot. He tried to teach me how to put more intensity into my voice, and we often worked on legato singing, the be-all and end-all of bel canto.

As Helmut Deutsch reports, your work with Hans Hotter was less successful.
It was a masterclass at the Richard Strauss Festival in Garmisch. Hotter was still of imposing stature even when sitting next to Helmut at the piano, striking the notes with his enormous hands and working away like a sculptor on every nuance, every word and every letter. He called it a 'consonantal legato', by which he meant that within a phrase the vowels should be linked by imaginary slurs and not interrupted by the intervening consonants. The little suffixes on individual words should lend the emotions even further scope for expression. It was from Richard Strauss that Hotter had learnt this careful handling of the words. I thought I understood what he meant, but unfortunately the chemistry between us didn't work. Each time I was about to sing out, he would interrupt me, insisting on a 'heartfelt and quiet basic tone', even in those passages in Strauss's songs that in my view demand the grand gesture of an operatic voice and a sound that fills the whole room.

Can you still remember what happened on Wednesday, 22 June 1994?
Yes, of course, it was my final exam in concert singing, a public concert comprising a selection of Strauss lieder, Schumann's

Dichterliebe and 'La donna è mobile' as an encore. Everything went well, and with that my studies were officially over.

Margarete Joswig

Then, in September 1994, you were released into the wild in order to begin your working life as a jack-of-all-trades at the Saarland State Theatre in Saarbrücken. What was your first impression?
Of the town? Well, what do you expect someone who grew up in Munich to say? But as an operatic novice starting your first real full-time job, you naturally have other worries: what is the atmosphere like in the company? What will your colleagues be like? From the outset I had a good feeling about it, and I wasn't wrong. For the most part, there was a family atmosphere, and fortunately I wasn't the only singer who was just starting out there. The other was Margarete Joswig. We began by eyeing each other critically. 'Why all this Italian machismo?' was Margarete's first impression of me. 'Hair gel, hip sunglasses, his car keys in his hand – and a mobile phone, of course. Arrives late but still manages to stroll in with the most incredible nonchalance. So typical of a tenor!' At the time she was less concerned with her own appearance and wore jumpers that she'd knitted herself. To begin with I thought she was a tree-hugger. Why didn't she wear something smarter, I wondered? Not even her fans recognized her when, after a performance of *Carmen*, they waited at the stage door to see the vivacious, hot-blooded gypsy whom they'd just admired onstage.

It wasn't long, however, before we saw behind the façade and discovered who we really were. We cooked meals together, went on excursions, chiefly to neighbouring France, and became close friends. From the very beginning I liked her sense of humour, and I appreciated her honesty. She never pretended to be anything other than the person she was. I could also tell her all about my problems, especially the first signs of my vocal crisis. At that time we were both seeing other people, and it never occurred to either of us that anything more could come of our friendship. Later we often laughed when we thought of the stage rehearsals in which we were physically very close. It was like the pop song 'Tausendmal berührt, tausendmal ist nichts passiert!' ('Touched a thousand times, a thousand times nothing happened!') But I still remember very clearly that when, in June 1996, I made up my mind to leave Saarbrücken and we were sitting together, surrounded by all my packing cases and drinking a glass of red wine, we suddenly realized that we didn't want to lose one another.

Saarbrücken

The galley years

The term 'galley years' has been used in opera at least since the time of Verdi, who coined it to describe the period in his life before his great breakthrough with *Rigoletto* in 1851, while Marilyn Horne used it as a chapter heading in her reminiscences of her years as a soprano in Gelsenkirchen from 1957 to 1960. This may sound like a gross exaggeration but it hits the nail on the head just as accurately now as it did fifty or two hundred years ago: for a beginner, the daily routine of life in an opera house can be grim. Auditioning is already bad enough, but the acid test comes later. Singers are thrown in at the deep end and have to learn to swim. Many drown, while others have to spend a long time treading water. Singers trained in Germany at least know that only in the most exceptional cases will they really be prepared for life in the theatre. Many a teacher and student complains about it, but to no avail. It is no wonder, then, that German singers generally fare worse in competitions and auditions than their rivals from the United States, Russia, China and Korea.

A main problem for beginners is how to organize their time when studying a role. While still at college they are used to spending months rehearsing suitable roles and preparing to sing them onstage. In the actual world of opera, they may well be caught unawares: if a singer falls ill, then his or her replacement has to learn the part in the shortest possible time. Every beginner is asked to be a jack-of-all-trades. Contracts are couched in such terms that the singer may be used anywhere – in roles that no one else wants to sing and in places that no one else wants to visit. From two o'clock on the previous day, singers can see from the relevant notices on the company's whiteboard when they are rehearsing a particular role and with whom. Unlucky singers may spend weeks attempting to escape from the treadmill of this routine.

Between chimneys and motorway

Jonas Kaufmann, too, found that his early years as a professional were a hard grind. In Saarbrücken he sang every tenor role that was going, from Nemorino in Donizetti's *L'elisir d'amore* to the Third Squire in *Parsifal* and from Andres in Berg's *Wozzeck* to Offenbach's *Die beiden Blinden* (*Les deux aveugles*). In the longer term he couldn't face the burdens placed on him, with the result that he was often ill. Although the chimneys of the coal-fired power stations did not emit as much smoke in 1994 as they had done in the days when coal production had met the bulk of the country's energy needs, the air quality in Saarbrücken remained distinctly poor. 'The fact that the Saarland had more forests than any other part of the Federal Republic was of little use to us in Saarbrücken,' recalls Margarete Joswig. 'It was quite simply an unhealthy environment. Not far from the theatre there's a beautiful park beyond which flows the Saar, while on the opposite bank are the Saar Meadows and then the motorway. And close by is a thermal power station. Even today I can still see the following surreal scene in my mind's eye: I'm pregnant, we're having a barbecue in the meadows. Friends and colleagues are lying stretched out on the grass and trying to relax between the coal-fired power station and the motorway.

But there was nothing else in the vicinity. The people at the theatre were extremely kind, especially the members of the chorus and the stage crew, and in general I found the working atmosphere agreeable. But everything was overshadowed by the fact that people around us were often ill, which with the passage of time naturally led to conflict. A lot was demanded of Jonas, largely with regard to the sheer amount of work that was expected of him. No one at that time recognized his vocal and artistic potential. And in the longer run this left him feeling frustrated.'

Both singers found themselves onstage together on the very first day of the new season for rehearsals for a new production of *Carmen* in which Margarete Joswig was one of Carmen's female friends, Mercédès, while Jonas Kaufmann was one of the smugglers, Remendado.

'At that date he was still a true *Spieltenor*,' recalls Barbara Hahn, the Carmen in this production, 'a singer cast in light tenor roles in operettas and in comic operas with spoken dialogue. He was in his mid-twenties and still unsure of his voice, also a little inhibited. He wasn't happy in Saarbrücken since he often had to sing things that didn't suit him vocally and that he still couldn't manage technically. And he was often ill. When I heard him again in Zurich ten or twelve years later, it almost blew me away. An incredible development had taken place in terms of both voice and personality – there was no comparison.'

Overexertion and vocal crisis

But Kaufmann first had to deal with a crisis. By his second year in Saarbrücken he had reached the point where he was thinking of giving up singing altogether.

Were you prepared for what hit you in Saarbrücken?
Absolutely not. When I turned up to meet the company, I had just left the removal boxes in my new place. I thought it would be a relaxed meeting, where we could get to know one another and afterwards I'd be able to return to my flat and unpack. I was all the more flabbergasted when we set to work straight away. I was coming from a completely different world. At college and in the opera studio no one had meant us any harm. Everyone had wanted to help us pull through. Not that this meant that we could sit back and do nothing. We had lots of subsidiary subjects to study: ballet, fencing, aural training and so on. But we had only two singing lessons a week, each of them lasting forty-five minutes. Of course, this was far too little.

And what about additional private lessons?
That was strictly forbidden. Anyone who broke this rule and was caught risked expulsion.

Sounds absurd.
Well, I can partly understand why. If I'm a teacher who's training a very gifted singer, I wouldn't find it so great if that singer was wooed away from me by someone who then put the icing on my cake and proudly hailed the result as his own 'discovery'. But it's a fact that two lessons a week aren't enough, no matter how good the teacher may be. Professional singing is an extremely physical affair, a competitive sport. And, as with every competitive sport, you've got to train every day. But if you do so without supervision, you generally run the risk of cultivating your mistakes and defects instead of getting rid of them. So the crux was that I had far too little time with my 'trainer'. That in itself explains why my college training was no preparation for daily professional life.

Even so, college gives you a chance to study entire roles.
But even this has little to do with actual practice, when things get serious. I don't know what it's like now, but in my day we had a whole year to study a new role. There would then be a production at the end of the summer term, by which time we'd already spent six months rehearsing onstage. So we were able to prepare our roles very calmly and ensure that vocally and physically they were second nature to us. In Saarbrücken I had to learn my roles in the shortest imaginable time, and this meant that I eventually came to grief. If you've got to con-jure a new character out of thin air overnight and you can't translate this into vocal terms straight away, this is extremely dangerous for the voice. Then there's the daily switch from one *Fach* to another. I had a contract typical of most beginners. It said: 'Tenor for opera, operetta, musicals depending on the character of the individual concerned', which meant 'Tenor for everything'. Someone said to me at the time: 'If you survive this, you'll easily manage the rest.' Perhaps I should have been more defensive, but with the exception of a single role I sang everything in Saarbrücken that I was required to sing.

And you were on the point of throwing it all in.
It was at a performance of *Parsifal* at which I sang the part of the Third Squire, a bit part if ever there was one. Around me were nothing but Wagnerian voices, and I naturally didn't want to sound like a gnat in comparison. So I really gave it my all – and within a few phrases I was completely hoarse. I opened my mouth and all that came out was hot air, my voice simply failed me. The conductor looked up at me in astonishment. For a singer, this is a nightmare, of course. It was the first time that I'd actually thought of giving up: 'If this is the professional life of a singer and if you have to go out on stage each evening suffering this degree of stress, I'd rather do something else, I won't do this to myself.' Today I know the reason: I didn't relax

and let my voice flow freely because I'd been trained to produce this 'German sound'.

Did you yourself want to sound like that? Or was this the ideal sound that you'd been taught to aspire to during your lessons?
Both. Both in my head and at college there was a set idea about what a German tenor should sound like. You had to fit into this mould, which had been shaped by singers like Peter Schreier. Of course, I'd like to have sounded like Fritz Wunderlich or Franco Corelli, but I thought that this was presumptuous of me and that I should be realistic. Whenever I subsequently felt the urge to let rip, I was immediately called to heel. My whole training could be summed up in the words: 'Just be careful and sing quietly, otherwise you'll ruin your voice. And if you're sensible, you may be able to sing Belmonte when you're forty.' It was according to this precept that I used my voice. And because I generally sang with a high larynx, I had no low notes, not even an F above middle C, let alone middle C itself. Among singers there is the saying: 'If he had at the top what he lacks at the bottom, he'd have a good middle register.' That's more or less what it was like with my voice.

And was there no one to correct you?
The only person who said anything was Josef Metternich. He was then seventy, a nice fellow in trainers who had a tremendous energy about him. At the very first lesson that I had with him he said: 'Listen, lad, I'm going to awaken the beast in you. Once it's been let out, it'll never go back in its box!' But at the time I didn't understand what he meant. The exercises that he set me were brutal – by the end of each lesson I was completely hoarse. But I continued to see him over quite a long period of time.

Presumably you needed to have been singing professionally for a number of years before you could have understood what he meant.

Maybe. It's now clear to me what he wanted. And it's enough to listen to his recordings to know what it sounds like when the 'beast has been wakened'. The way he trumpets the Verdi arias, with this incredibly concentrated sound and an almost tenoral ping at the top – that's something I've only ever heard in the recordings by the great Italian singers from the past.

What happened after the trauma of your Parsifal?

A dear colleague, the bass Greg Ryerson, took me to one side and said: 'I think you still need a bit more instruction. Come and see my teacher. I'm sure he'll be able to help.' And so, in Trier, I met the man to whom I basically owe everything: Michael Rhodes.

A turning point

Lessons with Michael Rhodes

The tale of Michael Rhodes and Jonas Kaufmann is a series of strokes of the greatest good fortune. It begins twenty-two years before Kaufmann was born.

It was in 1947 that Rhodes, a gifted young baritone from Brooklyn, made his debut at the New York City Opera. He had been born in the same hospital as Maria Callas – he was her elder by only four months – and first saw the light of day in August 1923. From an early age he heard and saw all the great singers at the Metropolitan Opera. After trying his luck in Lee Strasberg's acting school, where one of his fellow students was Marlon Brando, he realized that his great passion was music. Throughout his years with the New York City Opera, he naturally had his eye on the Met, but there the great baritone roles were already divided up between Leonard Warren and the young Robert Merrill. His colleague George London advised him to move to Europe, where there were many more opportunities. Rhodes followed London's advice and enjoyed a respectable career, singing in Berlin, where he also appeared with Callas and Karajan during La Scala's visiting performances of *Lucia di Lammermoor*, at the Paris Opéra, at La Scala, in Brussels, Amsterdam, Rome and Moscow. It was during a guest appearance in Trier that he met the love of his life, a teacher. The couple married and he moved to Trier. And so it came about that in 1995 he and Kaufmann were only an hour's car ride apart.

It was also a stroke of good fortune that Rhodes had been schooled in the technique associated with the name of Giuseppe De Luca, one of the twentieth century's leading baritones and singing teachers. It was from De Luca that Rhodes learnt the basis of his vocal technique: a wide placement of the larynx and the ability to allow the voice to flow freely without any tension. What this sounds like at its best emerges from De Luca's recordings, which include duets with Caruso. And in light of the fact that De Luca appeared in leading roles at the Met for twenty-two consecutive seasons and was still in full possession of his abilities at the time of his farewell concert in 1947, when he was seventy-three, we may conclude that this technique not only favoured a relaxed tone production but also contributed to the singer's vocal longevity.

Jonas Kaufmann was able to hear this for himself during one of his very first lessons with Rhodes and was both astonished and intimidated by the sounds that the baritone, who had already turned seventy, was able to produce when he needed to ascend into the tenor register. As one of the last singers to bridge the generations from the golden age of singing, as represented by Caruso, De Luca, Amato and Stracchiari, to today's generation of singers, Rhodes was an altogether exceptional singer. And for Jonas Kaufmann he became a saviour. The technique that the American baritone had learnt from De Luca and that he passed on to his own pupils not only helped Kaufmann to overcome his vocal crisis, it opened the door to an international career. Naturally even the best singing method still requires hard work and intelligence, but Jonas Kaufmann proved an exceptionally quick learner.

His first lesson took place on 23 August 1995. 'It was a very difficult time for him,' Michael Rhodes recalled some years later. 'He was in the midst of a vocal crisis. He was vocally inhibited and tense, his voice having been kept artificially small. But in spite of this you could hear what he had in him. When I told him that he'd one day be singing Lohengrin, he just stared at me in disbelief. But he realized what was involved far more quickly than most singers. He then came the following week and after that more and more often. Sometimes he would come on successive days. This went on for three years, and during that time he became like a son to me and my wife. The speed with which he could learn something new became clear to me while we were working together on his role in Romberg's *The Student Prince*. Anyone hearing him today would think that he was always able to speak perfect English, but this was by no means the case at that time. He learnt to speak an idiomatic English in the shortest possible time. His vocal progress could also soon be heard, especially in the world premiere of Antonio Bibalo's *The Glass Menagerie* here in Trier. I was absolutely sure that he'd manage it, which is why I advised him not to extend his contract in Saarbrücken. For outsiders this may have looked like a risky step, but it was the right one. At least since the time of his Jaquino in *Fidelio* in Stuttgart it was clear that he was on the right path. And from then on he took giant leaps forward. Now he is right at the top, and I believe he'll remain there for a very long time.'

However close Kaufmann had been to Michael Rhodes and his wife, the three of them saw each other only rarely in the years following the relaunch of his career. He was constantly on the road, singing in Stuttgart, Frankfurt, Klagenfurt, Brussels, Hamburg, Wiesbaden, Edinburgh and Vienna. But they remained in contact by telephone, and Anna and Michael Rhodes followed Kaufmann's career with a feeling of parental pride. The three met for the last time in early June 2011 after Kaufmann and Margarete Joswig had made a guest appearance together in Saarbrücken, performing Mahler's *Das Lied von der Erde* in the city's E-Werk. Michael Rhodes died in March 2013 at the age of eighty-nine. His obituary in the *Trierer Volksfreund* noted how fame came to him late in life. Fifteen years after their meeting in Saarbrücken in 1995, Jonas Kaufmann wrote in his autobiography that his teacher Michael Rhodes had been the 'turning point' in his life as a singer. As a consequence, 'Rhodes, who was otherwise retiring by nature, found himself in his old age the unexpected focus of attention in the big, wide world of opera'.

'Stop manipulating your voice'

Was there something like a key experience during the early part of your work with Michael Rhodes?
Right at the beginning. I auditioned for him, and he came straight to the point: 'You're simply not using your voice and instead singing as you imagine a lyric tenor should sound. Stop manipulating your voice. Just let it out.' This was the first time that anyone had put their finger on the problem – and for me it was like a moment of release. I'd been trained as a light, bright tenor and sang using head voice, producing a bright sound but 'holding on' to my voice too much and not allowing it to flow freely. Of course, I needed time to get used to the broad, dark sound that came out as soon as I opened up the back of my throat – as you do with a relaxed yawn. But I soon noticed that it was the right way. Previously I'd been used to my voice growing tired even during a lesson, but with Rhodes I had the feeling even after two and a half hours that I could go on singing for several more. Suddenly singing was no longer a burden but struck me as very straightforward. Rhodes showed me an entirely new way of handling my voice: much more physical, much more relaxed and also much more powerful. I'm so grateful to him for the fact that I'm still singing today.

Is it possible to explain the essence of vocal technique in a way that a lay person can understand?
Yes, I think so. In general, you have to ensure that your larynx is relaxed, that the shape of your mouth is correct and that your tongue doesn't get in the way. Your diaphragm must be pointing down and your back must be straight – then the air column, too, is straight. Then you create resonance and your voice can flow freely. Those are roughly the physical requirements. Purely in terms of your posture, then, it's not so difficult. The hardest part consists in overcoming physical and psychological blocks. You have to stop tinkering with your voice and wanting to sing things that simply don't suit your instrument. Only when you understand this will you find your voice. And then it's a question of refining it.

Among singers it's often said of voice coaches that you can be happy if they don't cause you any lasting harm.
That's no doubt true. It's an enormous stroke of good fortune to find someone like Michael Rhodes who can really help you and with whom you can make tremendous progress.

Why is it so hard to find a good teacher?
Many singers would say that it's because there are very few good teachers. Perhaps there's some truth in that remark.

Is it perhaps also because there is no vocal technique that suits every singer? Quite simply because we are all different? One singer may have a swan-like neck, the next no neck at all. How can the same method produce the desired result in both cases?
I see things differently. Of course, a teacher needs to take account of his or her students' different body types, just as he or she takes account of different types of voice – after all, the one affects the other. But I do think that there's a technique that's right for everyone. The basic elements – the position of the jaw,

tongue, thorax, diaphragm, larynx and trachea – should be the same with everyone. This needs to be tailored to the individual type only when the imagination comes into play. If you say something like, 'Yawn at the back of your throat' or 'Imagine a ball bouncing on top of a fountain', to one singer this will be as clear as mud, while another will grasp it at once. You often understand certain images and statements only much later. Take the exercise: 'Lift up the grand piano and sing.' In most cases a description like this proves meaningless. Only when you've seen removal men do it – activating the diaphragm and consciously breathing deeply – can you understand what is meant by this.

You completely revised your vocal technique as a result of your lessons with Rhodes, but didn't this lead to conflicts in your day-to-day work in Saarbrücken?
It certainly did! Within myself too. If you change your technique and are convinced that you've now found a solution to all your problems, you inevitably run the risk of lurching from one extreme to the other. Take the instruction: 'Open your throat right up at the back as if you were yawning.' Initially I took this to exaggerated lengths. I first had to find the happy medium. On the other hand, the principle of 'Always remain relaxed' was something I could easily put into practice. Don't increase the pressure when the tone is supposed to get bigger and fuller because that way you end up squashing it. What you need to do is relax even more and ensure that the jaw remains loose, that you breathe as deeply as possible and hold yourself in such a position that there is a straight line from your coccyx to your neck. This produces a long column of air in which the tone can develop. Changing a 'bright, head voice' to something 'broad and dark' was more or less like changing from a VW Beetle to a truck. You think it's the first time that you've driven and are correspondingly insecure. It was a strain on my nerves, but I

knew instinctively that this was the right way for me to achieve my goal and that I'd finally found the right vehicle.

Did your colleagues in the theatre think so, too?
Absolutely not. 'Artificially widened and darkened, discoloured vowels – it's the end!' Although not everyone said it in so many words, this was more or less the unanimous view at the theatre in Saarbrücken. Even Margarete was seriously unenthusiastic and it took her a long time to accept my soft singing. When singing soft notes I didn't want to switch to a purely lyrical head register but wanted to sing them with the same width with which I sing every other dynamic level. She didn't like this at all, and it was a long time before our views started to coincide on this point. The first three months of the new season were an unending ordeal. It was a difficult transitional period – I was sometimes able to put what I'd learnt into practice and apply it to a single phrase, only to relapse into old habits with the very next phrase. This happened with my first Don Ottavio in *Don Giovanni*. There were a few notes in the arias that struck people as positive, but there was also a lot that was wrong. In the ensembles, for example, I didn't have the right support because I thought I needed to save myself there. But I very soon noticed that exactly the opposite is true: if you spend the ensembles walking on tiptoes, as it were, you can't really run properly afterwards. But if you sing with full support, you can manage the rest without difficulty. This point later proved to be well founded when I sang *Così fan tutte* at the Piccolo Teatro in Milan: saving your voice is far more strenuous than fully supporting it.

What did people mean when they accused you of 'discolouring' your vowels?
I was looking for the right vocalic balance. If a phrase is to really sound legato, the vowels need to be balanced. In the German

school of singing the vowel 'i' generally stands out from the line as a fairly strident colour – it took a lot of time and effort for me to take this in hand because my jaw immediately made the old mistake of adopting the position needed for a 'narrow' sound. Singing 'a' but thinking 'i' is the secret of vocalic balance. But it took me a long time to get there. Today it's automatic, and whenever people compliment me on my diction, I'm immensely pleased because this means that my vowels are no longer discoloured.

A fresh start as a freelance artist

What happened next in Saarbrücken?
It's standard practice in the theatre to learn at the start of the season whether your contract has been renewed. The theatre needs to write to you by the middle of October, telling you whether your contract has been extended or not. And if you yourself want to end your contract, you have to do so by 30 October. My contract wasn't terminated, so I asked myself whether or not I wanted to stay. I spoke to the general manager and suggested the following: either I'd be given parts that were right for me during the coming season, or he'd allow me to accept guest engagements. And if neither of these alternatives was possible, then at least I wanted more money. He offered me an extra 100 marks because at that point he could promise me no specific roles as the new schedule still hadn't been finalized. 'All right,' I said, 'in that case I'd like to delay the date on which I can terminate my contract until you know which pieces may be coming my way.' He agreed, and when the new programme came out in March 1996 and it had nothing to offer as far as I was concerned, I handed in my notice without having anywhere else to go.

Fairly risky...

Of course. And not good for one's self-esteem. A twenty-seven-year-old can still return home and live with his parents if all else fails, but naturally you don't want to admit defeat. I don't know if I was thinking so far ahead at that time. I just wanted to escape from the treadmill. So I called my manager, Christian Lange, and told him of my decision to leave the company. 'Well, you've finally understood,' he said, 'it was never the right place for you.' What he meant was that I prefer to be my own boss. I need a certain degree of freedom and don't like it when other people plan my life for me and fill up my diary. I then become defensive and resistant. It can go so far as to make me ill. This was one of the reasons why I was so often ill in Saarbrücken. But when I myself am the idiot filling up my own diary, then I'm prepared to take the consequences of my actions and put up with it. I can't then tell myself: 'Look what they're expecting me to do!' That's also why I don't like it if people plan every last detail of my promotional activities and tell me that I have to give twelve interviews of half an hour each in the course of a day, since I already know in advance that there'll never be enough time for this.

So you became a freelance singer in the summer of 1996. Did you have to struggle financially?

Thanks to Christian Lange some good concerts came my way, as did a number of stage productions that I owed to a fortunate turn of events: Romberg's *The Student Prince* at the Heidelberg Castle Festival, *Don Giovanni* at the Goethe Theatre in Bad Lauchstädt and Antonio Bibalo's *The Glass Menagerie* in Trier. All of them were lifelines – exactly what I needed to consolidate my existence and to build up my self-confidence. Meanwhile I was also making excellent progress in my work with Michael Rhodes. He got me to sing the whole of Don Carlo and even parts of Otello. I was finally able to explore my true potential.

Even so, I still looked at him in disbelief when he said: 'One day you'll sing at La Scala and at the Met.' On his concert grand piano he had a tear-off pad from the Met's shop. On every page it read: 'Don't forget the Met!'

Rhodes said that even at this period it was already possible to hear your vocal potential – in The Glass Menagerie *in Trier, for example.*

I certainly felt comfortable within myself. The character that I was playing was a laid-back sort of person who also functions as the narrator. This laid-back nature of the character undoubtedly helped me to be more relaxed when singing. It was also a world premiere, so there were no models on which to base our performances, no recordings, no influences, no vocal image of this part – and so I was able to shape it to suit my own style and abilities. It was also the first time that I discovered my delight in acting. True, I'd often been to the theatre as a child, both the Residenztheater and the Kammerspiele; I'd seen Therese Giehse, Thomas Holtzmann, Peter Lühr and all the greats, but until then I'd never really trusted myself as an actor. Now I suddenly had a lot of text to work on and realized to my surprise that it was actually a good deal of fun.

Did you receive any more offers of a full-time permanent contract?

Yes, I received two. One from Stuttgart, and an earlier one from Würzburg. I'd auditioned there for a new production of *Die Zauberflöte* – or so I thought. In fact it was for a permanent post with the company. After the audition had passed off so well, they wanted to discuss a full-time contract with me. 'No, nothing permanent, I just want to sing Tamino.' They became almost angry as they already had two singers for Tamino. But the director of *Die Zauberflöte* said: 'Then give him a contract just for this piece.' The rehearsals began and they were a lot of fun. Diana Damrau was also in the cast – in fact it was her first engagement – as Papagena on roller-skates. We'd been rehearsing for three weeks, but there was still no sign of a contract, so I went to see the general manager: 'How many performances am I singing?' – 'It depends entirely on how expensive you are.' Very well, I thought, for a good concert I can get 3,000 marks, so I need to drop my price; '1,800 marks,' I said. 'For that I can give you precisely one performance, the first night. I can't afford any more.' And so it came about that I sang just one Tamino in Würzburg. But my sense of frustration didn't last long. In April 1997 I received a call from the State Opera in Stuttgart asking me if I would have time for two new productions: Szymanowski's *King Roger* in a production by Peter Mussbach and *Fidelio* directed by Martin Kušej. These were my first experiences of 'music theatre'. But that's a chapter unto itself.

Music theatre

~~

Protest at the opera

According to the director, Liù – the slave girl in Puccini's *Turandot* – has to sing her first-act aria, 'Signore, ascolta', as if she is Mata Hari: old Timur has ordered her to seduce the Unknown Prince in order to uncover his secret. The singer submits to the inevitable, divests herself of various articles of clothing and sets to work on her tenor colleague, only for him to send her packing. She ends her aria with its difficult final phrase, 'Ah, pietà', producing a magnificent *messa di voce* on the very last note: it is an extremely respectable vocal achievement. Members of the audience raise their hands to applaud, but before they can do so, Liù receives a resounding slap across the face from Timur. He is evidently dissatisfied with the result of her attempt to seduce the Unknown Prince. The shocked silence is interrupted by a cry from the audience: 'Hey, she wasn't all that bad!' Laughter and hesitant applause are interspersed by shouts of protest. A minor scandal at the opera.

This scene took place at the Aalto Theatre in Essen in 2007 and is typical of a phenomenon known as *Regietheater*, literally 'directors' theatre'. Its aim, among others, is to provoke. The 'indolent, elderly audience' has to be stirred into life, the press needs something to write about, and no one can say that nothing is happening in opera. Catcalls from the audience and a chorus of boos for the production team are an integral part of the performance, and if everything goes to plan, the town has its latest theatrical scandal. And the apparent success of the exercise seems to suggest that the organizers are right: people are finally going to the opera who would otherwise never dream of doing so. As a result, everyone is now a part of the game: general managers and conductors just as much as singers and journalists. Privately, they continue to say what they really think about the production, but in public they give away as little as possible: not so much because they fear for their jobs but because they are afraid of being applauded by the wrong side, namely, the conservative reactionaries and *laudatores temporis acti*. Better, then, to be open to innovation. And how often have productions that triggered a wave of violent protest in their first year been acclaimed as pioneering when revived in subsequent seasons? Think only of Chéreau's centennial *Ring* in Bayreuth.

This, then, is the one extreme. The other may be termed 'Grandad's Opera'. This type of opera assumes the form of concerts in costume and make-up, singers lined up by the footlights and belting their arias straight out into the auditorium. 'Park and bark' is a phrase often used in this context. This is not something that anyone seriously interested in opera wants. A discontinued line, it offers no real alternative to *Regietheater*.

Between these two extremes lies a wide and varied field where 'music theatre' – to use the term that came into circulation in the late 1950s – may ideally be able to flourish in the form of a creative combination of music and drama. One precondition of this art form is for both the conductor and the director to want the same thing and the singers see themselves as singing actors. A good example of this type of music theatre is Willy Decker's Salzburg production of *La traviata* with Anna Netrebko and Rolando Villazón that was broadcast on television in 2005, when it attracted a surprisingly large number of viewers. Unlike many new productions, this reading of *La traviata* was not a concert performance with a few extra touches added by a director from the world of the spoken theatre but a highly successful blend of music and theatre.

The Stuttgart Opera

For a long time the Stuttgart Opera was regarded as a veritable hotbed of music theatre. In 1997–8 – the season in which Jonas Kaufmann sang his first roles there – it was voted Opera House of the Year by the German trade journal *Opernwelt*. The lead article featured a still from the company's new production of Szymanowski's *King Roger*, with Wolfgang Schöne in the title role, a production voted the season's most important revival of a forgotten work. The production also marked Lothar Zagrosek's debut as the house's new general music director, while Jonas Kaufmann was nominated as Young Singer of the Year for his portrayal of the Arab scholar Edrisi.

'Even at this point Jonas was already a singer who immediately caught your attention,' Wolfgang Schöne recalls. 'At the end of the first rehearsal, I said to Pamela Rosenberg: "You really must sign him up." Unfortunately I heard him only infrequently after *King Roger*. But when I did hear him again onstage after a lengthy period of time, as Des Grieux in Chicago in 2008, opposite Natalie Dessay as Manon, I was completely bowled over. His voice had developed in ways that I've not known with any other singer during the whole of my professional career. And then there was this incredible ability to sing softly in Des Grieux's "Ah! fuyez, douce image". I was completely enthralled and imagined how wonderful it would be if he were to sing Lohengrin with these vocal resources.'

The artistic profile of the Stuttgart Opera was shaped by two people who complemented one another in an altogether ideal way: a first-rate dramaturge, Klaus Zehelein saw his role first and foremost as a man of the theatre, while the musical side of the company was overseen by Pamela Rosenberg, who later became the general manager at the San Francisco Opera. Zehelein and Rosenberg ran the Stuttgart company from 1991 to 2000, and during that time they attracted the premier league of avant-garde directors, including Ruth Berghaus, Hans Neuenfels, Christof Nel, Johannes Schaaf and Peter Mussbach. It was Mussbach who directed *King Roger*, although his production was not a success; *Opernwelt*, for example, opining that it had prevented audiences from appreciating the little-known work rather than revealing it in all its glory. The rehearsal period, too, was an unhappy one, starting with a meeting at which the director explained his concept, only for the participants to ask what Mussbach's explanations had to do with the piece itself. When the costume designer announced that she had not yet produced any designs because she first wanted to get to know the singers, Wolfgang Schöne retorted: 'In other words, you haven't done your homework.' An embarrassed silence followed. 'Then I suggest we all go home and not return until you've come up with some ideas.'

So this was your first experience of music theatre...
Not entirely. My very first experience was in Saarbrücken with Berg's *Wozzeck* and Schoenberg's *Moses und Aron*, both of them directed by Christian Pöppelreiter. He had learnt to play the viola and so he understands music. During one rehearsal he told us: 'I have in my head a film of the work – I hope you do, too. We'll edit the best possible version from this.' He prepared himself in great detail and knew exactly what he wanted, but he was always ready to take note of the performer's individuality and find a common solution. Mussbach's production of *King Roger* remained a mystery to me right up to the end. He never showed his cards and parried all our questions. I was all the more taken with my next production in Stuttgart, Martin

Kušej's *Fidelio*. He'd previously directed Purcell's *King Arthur* in Stuttgart; I'd seen it and liked it a lot. He has a phenomenal ability to create a coherent whole out of the singers, actors and dancers. His production of *Fidelio* was one of the best examples of music theatre I've ever seen.

Martin Kušej's production of Fidelio

You didn't sing Florestan but the smaller tenor role of Jaquino. How did Kušej conceive this part?

He made it much more important. Instead of the minor official whom you normally see, Kušej showed us a power-hungry brute of a man: after Jaquino catches Marzelline canoodling with Fidelio, he rapes her over the washstand. And in Kušej's production he wasn't a porter but a prison guard. The walls of the prison were covered in wallpaper depicting a forest, and Jaquino played a tape featuring splashing waves and twittering birds. Kušej told us about a study indicating that suicide rates are far higher in prisons when the prisoners can see the world of nature and can glimpse freedom – in other words, if they are confronted every day with what has been taken away from them.

It is said that in this production there were excruciatingly long pauses in the spoken dialogue.

They lasted a maximum of two minutes. The conductor, Michael Gielen, timed them on his stopwatch. I liked this idea because it made the tension in the piece all the more palpable. But in an age of zapping such pauses were a trial. Many members of the audience grew impatient: 'Hey, what's up?' people called out from the auditorium. 'Has there been a power failure?'

How did Kušej stage the opera's principal problem area, the cele-bratory finale?

From the outset he had agreed with Gielen on this point: the celebrations are completely over the top. The more the characters repeat their hymn to marital love, the less we believe them. And so Kušej and Gielen concluded that the prisoners are liberated only in Leonore's imagination. Her decision to save Florestan is like a torpedo – once it has been fired, it inevitably finds its target. And when Leonore and Pizarro meet in the dungeon, the whole thing explodes. In a film, Kušej said, the cover of the cistern would give way and everyone would plunge down into the darkness. Throughout the rest of the opera their free fall would be shown in slow motion until just before the inevitable impact. His solution for presenting this scene onstage was for Leonore to press her pistol to Pizarro's temple, while Pizarro simultaneously holds his knife to Florestan's throat. At that point we hear the second fanfare. Pizarro slashes Florestan's throat, there is a spray of blood and a shot rings out. Deathly silence and total darkness. Hesitant applause, some members of the audience evidently thinking that the performance was over. Then unnatural neon lighting. The characters all look like zombies. Except for Leonore. She is the only person still alive. The rest of the opera is her fantasy, her vision.

Così fan tutte *with Giorgio Strehler*

Between King Roger *and* Fidelio *you took part in your first important production abroad:* Così fan tutte *directed by Giorgio Strehler at the new Piccolo Teatro in Milan.*

It came about only after several false starts. Strehler had very particular ideas about how to cast the work, and so auditions for it were held all over the world. I auditioned for him, in the old Piccolo Teatro, Edgardo's scene from *Lucia di Lammermoor* and, of course, Ferrando's aria, 'Un'aura amorosa'. After the very first phrase Strehler shouted, 'Stop. Kneel down and start again!' I did as I was bidden. 'Stop! Sing it with your eyes closed!' OK. When I'd finished, he said: 'We should do something together, perhaps *Lucia*, but not *Così*. You're too old for Ferrando.' I'd just turned twenty-seven at the time! But Strehler was determined to have very young people in his cast. His initial idea was that the performers who played the two couples should all be under twenty. That wasn't feasible, of course. The next threshold was twenty-five. But where can you find a decent Fiordiligi under twenty-five? So he kept having to move the age limit upwards, with the result that a few months later I received a phone call from Milan: 'Strehler has heard umpteen tenors, but he wants you!' The stupid thing was that by then I'd already signed the contract for *King Roger*, and the last two performances in Stuttgart were right in the middle of the rehearsals for *Così fan tutte*. So I turned him down, albeit with a heavy heart. I then received a fax, which said something along the lines of, 'I'm Giorgio Strehler. And when I call, you have to come.' To which I wrote back: 'And when I sign a contract, I stick to its terms.' To cut a long story short, we agreed that I could arrive late for the rehearsals. He greeted me in Milan with the words: 'It simply had to be.' His colleagues later quoted him as saying: 'Vabene, lavoriamoci il culo per questo Kaufmann!' ('Let's work our arses off for this Kaufmann!')

Why was it so important to him that both couples should be so young?
He wanted to ensure that when the characters toy with each other's feelings, it should be as believable as possible. 'Once you have a certain life experience,' he once said, 'you know how disillusioning and mortifying love can be. You then take greater care. But when you're young, you believe everything. And now imagine: two couples who live next door to each other go off

on holiday together and share everything. And at some stage the point comes when each of them wonders what it would be like to swap partners. Curiosity and fun turn to seriousness, leading in turn to conflict. No one wants to return to the original arrangement.' I find that very plausible. The piece gains in tragedy in consequence. In Strehler's production Alfonso and Despina, too, were a couple, a former couple. And the casting was spot on: Janet Perry and her former husband, Alexander Malta. Malta was fantastic, he was exactly the type that Strehler wanted, a man who has lived his life to the full without leaving anything out, a tramp with the wisdom of old age. This made absolute sense in this particular setup.

'Create something new each time'

Così fan tutte *was evidently Strehler's problem child. According to Walter Legge, he first wanted to stage it at the Piccola Scala as early as 1956, with Guido Cantelli on the podium and an all-star cast that included Elisabeth Schwarzkopf, Graziella Sciutti, Luigi Alva and Rolando Panerai. But 'at the sight of Eugene Berman's murky decor he stormed out of the theatre belching clouds of quadrilingual obscenities'.*

I didn't know that. I just sensed that he felt a tremendous respect for the work. It's also an extremely difficult piece to stage, above all on account of the scenes in which Ferrando and Guglielmo disguise themselves, since every member of the audience is bound to ask why the women don't recognize their menfolk. Working with Strehler was one of the great theatrical experiences of my life. What control this old man had, with his incredible energy and presence! We all felt as if we were still at school. His great credo was that the action onstage should be reinvented each evening. The performers should at all costs avoid a fixed routine and should never just reproduce the same old stage business. That was anathema to him. For Ferrando's second aria, 'Tradito, schernito', he spent an hour feeding me information and explaining the aria's emotions. 'That's the situation, that's how he feels. That's the essence. How you play it is a matter of indifference to me, the main thing is that the audience understands what's going on. And if you feel this scene differently tomorrow, then you need to do it differently, you must create something new each time.' For me this was new territory. Until then I'd been used to the director explaining every step to me. At the very least I needed a basic framework. Strehler taught me to create my own framework. Once I've done that, I can be spontaneous and, even more crucially, I can react spontaneously to what my partners are doing. For me, this was a revelatory experience, and I found the rehearsals so inspirational that the constant toing and froing between Milan and Stuttgart didn't bother me in the slightest. All the greater was my sense of shock when my manager rang me up on Boxing Day 1997 and said: 'Strehler's dead.' It was inconceivable; I felt so wretched that I couldn't even bring myself to travel to Milan for the funeral. I didn't want to see it. To have finally found such a man of the theatre . . . You should have seen him, this white-haired man with eyes glowing like coals and bursting with energy. If any of us made ourselves comfortable in a chair, he would become wild: 'You're young! Chop, chop! Get a move on!' He was a despot, a tyrant, but everyone did as they were told without grumbling. With his death we found ourselves in a vacuum. What was to be done? His assistants got the RAI technicians to send them the videos that a team of film-makers had made during the rehearsals. And these recordings were now treated as if they were a production book: 'Jonas! Move eight inches to your right! Stop! That's the position you were in at your last rehearsal with the maestro. Please stay there!' In short, it was the exact opposite of what Strehler himself had wanted.

What about the performances themselves? Were you able to implement any of the ideas that Strehler had taught you?
We certainly tried, and I do believe that on the whole it was in his spirit. In any case, no two performances were the same. We tried to avoid every kind of mechanical move. Whether we succeeded in reinventing the whole thing every evening is a question that I can't answer. Audiences liked it, and there was a tremendous run on the box office. Later we went on tour with the production. Among the places we visited were the Wiesbaden International May Festival and Japan.

La Scala debut

What happened next in Stuttgart?
I sang Almaviva in Rossini's *Barbiere*. That, too, went well. The next thing that Pamela Rosenberg gave me was Alfredo in *La traviata*. I had no experience of this repertory, and so it was a real demonstration of her faith in me. It was an existing production by Ruth Berghaus that really impressed me. And without knowing it at the time, I was laying the foundations for my later successes abroad. I next sang Jaquino at La Scala.

How did that come about?
The usual procedure: an Italian agency sent me to Milan to audition, but on the actual day it turned out that all of the other candidates had cancelled, so I found myself alone on the stage of La Scala. From somewhere out of the darkness, Riccardo Muti asked me if I could sing something by Lortzing. I had to say no. He then wanted to know if there was an interesting 'aria' in Jaquino's part. I had to say no to that, too. I was then allowed to sing the arias from *La traviata* and *Die Zauberflöte* that I'd brought with me. I guess it went well.

And what was it like to sing for the first time in these hallowed halls?

I don't normally get nervous, but I can still remember that at the start of the first performance, before the duet with Marzelline, my heart was in my mouth: I was standing on the stage of La Scala, where all the great singers had stood. For me, it had been an unattainable Olympus, but now my dream had come true.

Fidelio *with Rilling and Harnoncourt*

Barely three years later you graduated from the small role of Jaquino to the main tenor role in Fidelio, *Florestan. It's a part that's feared even by experienced heldentenors. Were you attracted to the part? Or was the invitation to sing it so enticing that you couldn't resist it?*

It all began with my appearing in various concerts under Helmut Rilling, including Haydn's *The Creation*. Rilling was evidently pleased with my performances. At all events, he asked me if I could imagine singing my first Florestan with him. I was rather sceptical and asked him if I could think it over. I first wanted to see if I could get through the part. So I went to visit my coach in Munich and placed the score in front of her. She became agitated: 'Put it away, it's not for you. Far too soon!' But then she allowed herself to be swayed, and so we spent hours working through the part, including four read-throughs of the difficult final section of the aria, in which many tenors have come to grief. We also worked through the duet twice, and so on. I think she'd really been intending to finish me off completely. 'What? You're still not hoarse?' she groaned at the end. 'All right then, do it!' There were three concert performances, one at the Rheingau Music Festival, another in the Stuttgart Liederhalle and the third at the Beethoven Festival in Bonn. And it all went really well. To my immense delight my voice didn't tighten up at the difficult passages but continued to open out.

Florestan's ecstatic vision of the angel that rescues him ('Der führt mich zur Freiheit ins himmlische Reich' / 'It guides me to freedom, to the kingdom of Heaven') is a fiendishly difficult phrase that is often cited as evidence of the claim that Beethoven didn't know how to write for singers. But it can also be interpreted as a conscious decision to drive the singer to the very limits of what is singable: the prisoner's extreme situation requires that extreme demands be placed on the singer.

I think it's the latter, because if you look at the *Missa solemnis* you can see very clearly that the idea of expressing despair through music that's unsingable is very much a part of the underlying concept, as in the phrase 'Et vitam venturi', in which the vocal line of the choral sopranos is ratcheted higher and higher.

But how do you manage to sing this phrase so you don't overstretch yourself?

For me, there is only one way, which is not to panic but to remain as relaxed as possible. And I also need to avoid getting ahead of myself in the hope of dealing more swiftly with the problem since that always achieves precisely the opposite by making the gaps between breaths even shorter. And this proved to be the right solution when I first sang Florestan onstage two years later in Zurich with Nikolaus Harnoncourt in a production directed by Jürgen Flimm.

The production has been preserved on DVD. It's hardly a pioneering interpretation of the work, but it has its powerful moments, notably Florestan's reaction to Leonore.

I thought this entirely plausible. Florestan is done with his life, he is waiting for death and starting to hallucinate, when a young man suddenly appears before him, claiming to be his wife. At this point Florestan is bound to think that he's lost it, so it's only logical that in his duet with Leonore, he repeats her words as if he is remote-controlled. He still can't believe it. This idea was well suited to the unusually slow tempo that Nikolaus Harnoncourt chose for this scene. In Flimm's production the final scene was entirely realistic: the women free their menfolk from their chains and Pizarro is shot by Jaquino while trying to escape.

The Salzburg Entführung

It is in the nature of music theatre that the quality fluctuates widely: every new production is made up of many different elements, most of which are barely calculable. Will the director's concept work out, for example? If not, the singers will find that they have been dealt a poor hand: they risk their necks, and if they are unlucky, they have to serve as lightning conductors for the audience's anger – just as you yourself did at the new production of Die Entführung aus dem Serail *at the 2003 Salzburg Festival.* Oh, that was brutal! I'd never known that an audience could be so hostile, at least as an active singer. We had the feeling that before the start of the performance a group of people had decided that they were going to go to the opera and cause a riot. They hated the production, and it was the singers who took a beating for it. At one point the shouting and whistling was so bad that I exploded: 'You're all free to leave!' I shouted. From that moment on it was impossible for me to set foot onstage without being greeted by a chorus of boos. The press carried reports along the lines of 'Singer antagonizes audience'.

To judge by what one reads in the press the scandal was predictable thanks to Stefan Herheim's production. What do you do if you feel that the director's concept runs completely against the grain? Do you discuss the matter, negotiate with the director or threaten to leave?

I try to find a face-saving solution that everyone can agree to. I don't think that walking out is a solution, because then you lose the chance of doing something new in opera. And it wouldn't help. All it would achieve is that you'd be labelled 'difficult'. In singers' lives, too, there are situations where you simply have to carry on with things that aren't your responsibility. It's the same with us as with everyone else who's part of the team. On the other hand, the director is already at home with his feet up by the time of the second performance, while the rest of us are still having to face the audience's indignation.

How did your Salzburg engagement come about?

Through Gerard Mortier, who was then the Festival's artistic director. I was rehearsing *La clemenza di Tito* in Klagenfurt – the pianist Stefan Vladar was conducting his first opera there and the director was Caroline Gruber – and I travelled to Salzburg to audition for him. He immediately signed me up for a small role in Peter Mussbach's production of Busoni's *Doktor Faust* with Thomas Hampson. That was my Salzburg Festival debut in the summer of 1999. In turn this led to my first contact with Bernd Loebe, who invited me to appear in a new production of *Die Entführung* in Brussels: a delightful staging by Christof Loy. Once Mortier had heard me in this production, he invited me to sing Belmonte in Salzburg, too.

Did you feel comfortable vocally with the part?

Certainly in Brussels, but I think that by the time I sang Belmonte in Salzburg four years later I'd outgrown the part. The lyrical sections passed off without difficulty, but I was no longer able to sing the ornamented passages with the ease that the role ideally demands. Loebe offered me a second production in

Brussels, and it was one which, musically speaking, was a huge success: Berlioz's *La damnation de Faust*. Susan Graham was the Marguerite, José van Dam the Méphistophélès. It was also the first time I'd worked with Tony Pappano, a thoroughbred musician and a theatre conductor par excellence. I should add that I fell in love with the piece straight away and have sung it on a number of other occasions, notably in a phenomenal production by Olivier Py in Geneva, also with Van Dam, immediately after the Salzburg *Entführung*.

Debuts in Chicago and Paris

When I look at the start of your international career, I have the impression that you pursued a particular strategy that involved not rushing your fences but beginning with smaller roles. That's certainly how it was at La Scala, the Salzburg Festival and your debuts in Chicago and Paris.

It wasn't a strategy to begin with but was simply the result of what I was offered and what was demanded of me. Not until Chicago and Paris did it become a strategy. While in Salzburg I auditioned for Bill Mason, the head of the Lyric Opera in Chicago, and he offered me Alfredo in a new production of *La traviata*. But this was too risky for me: I hadn't yet sung the role, and to do so in a house with 3,500 seats ... So I asked if it could be something else, resulting in my debut as Cassio in *Otello*. It wasn't until the revival in 2003 that I sang Alfredo in Chicago. By then I'd sung the part in Stuttgart and the vast space in Chicago had lost its terrors for me: I felt safe there. It was the same in Paris. There, too, I thought it better to start with Cassio, which was safer than risking exposure in a major role. Things worked out well, so that the next role I sang there was again Alfredo. This was also my next role at La Scala.

La rondine *in London*

Conversely, it was already a leading role in which you made your Covent Garden debut: Ruggero in a revival of Puccini's La rondine *with Angela Gheorghiu.*
That was the period when Angela Gheorghiu and Roberto Alagna had decided no longer to appear together. When Alagna withdrew from the revival of *La rondine*, Angela Gheorghiu mentioned my name. Tony Pappano, whom I'd gotten to know in Brussels, was now music director at Covent Garden, so there was nothing to stand in the way of my London debut. I should add that I owe a great deal to Angela.

What was it like, working with her for the first time?
Wonderful. We developed an instant rapport, and there were always surprises in our scenes together: she would do the same piece of business completely differently at consecutive performances, grinning at me in secret and watching to see how I'd react. I find this kind of spontaneous creativity hugely inspiring. And with revivals, when the director is no longer present and a production assistant is responsible for ensuring that a scene is performed in the spirit of its creator, you may not have the chance to work out something new with the ensemble but have to take note of the old production and assume qualities that another singer developed, which means that you're far more dependent on the spontaneity and creativity of your partners. In situations like this, all that Strehler taught us is essential. After all, music theatre stems not just from the concept of the director but at least in equal measure from the creative input of the performers.

Zurich as mother ship

Ensemble theatre

Anyone leafing through old programmes from German-speaking opera houses is likely to be overcome by feelings of nostalgia. Only a few months before Fritz Wunderlich made his role debut as Pfitzner's Palestrina at the Vienna State Opera on 16 December 1964, he had sung two cameo roles for the company: the Apparition of a Young Man in *Die Frau ohne Schatten* and the Italian Singer in *Capriccio*. The leading singers were part of an ensemble and bound to the house by contracts that guaranteed a fixed number of performances, often leading to luxury casting in minor roles.

In return these singers were allowed to undertake guest engagements once they had completed their allotted number of appearances in Vienna. During this period the Deutsche Oper in Berlin, the Vienna State Opera and the companies in Stuttgart and Munich were all home to many leading singers. And general managers of the old school such as Walter Erich Schäfer in Stuttgart followed the careers of their former protégés with paternalistic concern, allowing them to sing difficult parts at home before they risked possible disaster with a premature role debut in London or New York.

This is how things used to be. All that remains today of the old German ensemble theatres are the singers who take on secondary roles. Anyone who wants to sing major roles must decide whether he or she wants to remain a permanent member of a small or medium-sized house, with little time for guest appearances, or whether they travel the world as freelance artists. The older model of a mother ship offering singers a chance to embark on their international careers is now seen as outdated, although it continued to function well in a handful of individual companies, most recently in Zurich under the administration of Alexander Pereira. For over twenty years, from 1991 to 2012, Pereira was able to achieve what many men of the theatre had tried in vain to do before him, namely to keep together an ensemble of first-class singers, many of whom were in international demand, and to use them not only in new productions but also in repertory performances over the course of several seasons. Singers such as Vesselina Kasarova, Thomas Hampson, Cecilia Bartoli, Edita Gruberova and Peter Seiffert returned to Zurich on a regular basis, while others, such as Roberto Saccà, Michael Volle and Jonas Kaufmann pursued international careers with the Zurich Opera as their principal hub.

A prophet in his own country

In Kaufmann's case there was an additional factor that may be observed in the careers of many singers: a prophet has no honour in his own country. And yet everything could have turned out very differently: Kaufmann could have lived in Munich, sung at the Bavarian State Opera and used it as a base for guest appearances in music centres in the big wide world of opera. But this was not to be.

Kaufmann was invited to audition for the company in the wake of his successes in Stuttgart and Milan, but in spite of the encouragement that he received ('Wonderful! Magnificent!'), the only practical consequence was a single performance of *Così fan tutte* on 11 February 2001, when he took over at the last minute from an ailing colleague. And that was all. Kaufmann was understandably disappointed and sought the advice of Hermann Prey, whom he had gotten to know through his manager Christian Lange. Prey sought to mediate, but there was an obvious lack of chemistry between Kaufmann and his namesake, Sir Peter Jonas, who was then the company's general manager.

Conversely, Kaufmann had no complaints about Zurich, where his career was from the outset blessed by good fortune. His debut in June 1999 was a matinee made up of comic pieces by Mozart and was followed by a production of Ferdinando Paer's *Leonora*, which was staged in Zurich's outpost in Winterthur in September 2000. Remarkably, Paer's opera, which had first been seen in Dresden in October 1804, only a year before the first version of Beethoven's *Fidelio*, had never previously been staged in Switzerland, with the result that the production attracted international attention. The critic of the *Frankfurter Allgemeine Zeitung*, for example, noted that 'Florestan was sung by the Munich tenor Jonas Kaufmann, a singer with the now rarely found steely power necessary for heroic roles. Here the tenor has the opera's best bits to sing, and Kaufmann took uninhibited advantage of this.' *Opernwelt* used a striking photograph of Kaufmann for the cover of its November issue. Here, too, there was praise, albeit with an undertow of concern: 'There is no doubt that he is one of the most gifted lyric tenors of his generation. The burnished timbre is imme-diately lodged in the memory. Sometimes there is a hint of the heroism that appears to look forward to Beethoven's Florestan but which was never Paer's intention. Let us hope that he is not tempted down this road: if Kaufmann continues to stick to lyric roles, he will have no need to fear any rivals.'

Permanence and freedom

'But it's clear to you that I must have you,' Alexander Pereira said after the final dress rehearsal. Kaufmann was hesitant. On the one hand a permanent contract would give him the security that he needed as a young father, especially now that his wife had temporarily abandoned her operatic career following the birth of their first child, while on the other hand a permanent appointment was also a form of straitjacket. It was then that he was told by his Zurich colleague Oliver Widmer that a permanent contract in Zurich was very different from anything he had known previously, namely, a fixed number of performances and nothing more. 'I wasn't tied down for the whole season but could also decide what I would sing and what I wouldn't sing. And, of course, I was tempted by the prospect of living in Zurich with my family and of being only a couple of minutes away from the theatre. There's a difference between spending all of your time on the road and living out of a suitcase as a freelance singer and singing in a house where you really feel at home. You know every theatre technician, every orchestral musician, every member of the chorus and also your colleagues. You can try out roles when you're not entirely convinced that they're for you. And so Zurich became my haven for five years.'

A rollercoaster of emotions

Kaufmann's first performance in Zurich was as Tamino in *Die Zauberflöte* in October 2000. It marked the start of a whole series of disparate roles: Mozart's Belmonte, Ferrando, Idomeneo and Tito; Monteverdi's Telemaco and Nero; the title roles in Schubert's *Fierrabras*, Gounod's *Faust*, Wagner's *Parsifal* and Verdi's *Don Carlo*; Fenton in *Falstaff*, the Duke of Mantua in *Rigoletto* and Alfredo in *La traviata*; Florestan in *Fidelio* and Don José in *Carmen*; Cavaradossi in *Tosca* and the Prince in Humperdinck's *Königskinder*.

There were often periods which required vocal versatility: a run of *Don Carlo* might be followed by another Tamino, while he might find himself singing Parsifal, Alfredo and Fierrabras within a matter of days. But Kaufmann loved this rollercoaster of emotions, not just because it kept his voice flexible but also because the different styles, languages and tone colours had a positive impact on each other. For his international career, too, such variety and versatility could only be beneficial. It was impossible for foreign companies to label him a 'Mozart singer' or a 'German tenor'. Instead, they treated him as an individual artist and used him accordingly.

Kaufmann's vocal development kept pace with his growing repertory. When he heard himself as Fierrabras in a recording of one of the rehearsals for Schubert's opera, he asked: 'Is that me? It sounds really fat-toned!' The new production – later recorded and released on DVD – remains one of Kaufmann's fondest memories of Zurich: a powerful but neglected work in an impressive production by Claus Guth with a well-matched team of singers that included Michael Volle, Christoph Strehl and László Polgár under the baton of Franz Welser-Möst. The only regret is that the press expatiated at interminable length on the work and the production, while dismissing the singers in only a few words with attributes such as 'virile and dramatic' and 'warm-toned', followed by the names of the characters in parentheses.

A completely different note was struck by Werner Pfister two months later, when he reviewed Kaufmann's Idomeneo in the *Zürichsee-Zeitung* in mid-January 2003, hailing the tenor as 'such a thoughtful and subtly differentiated stylist that one hangs on his every word. Even the dynamic subtleties in his part deserve the highest praise; his relatively dark if at times strangely tangy timbre predestines him for this role, not least because he has no problems with the coloratura writing or with the top notes – he can even afford to perform the much-feared initial version of "Fuor del mar".'

Among the highlights of his years in Zurich, Kaufmann names not only his first fully staged performances of Florestan in *Fidelio* but also Monteverdi's *L'incoronazione di Poppea* (again with Harnoncourt and Flimm and with Vesselina Kasarova in the title role) and Humperdinck's *Königskinder* in a production by Jens-Daniel Herzog. 'During this period I also got to know lots of great conductors, including Nello Santi, a rock of reliability in the Verdi repertory. But the most formative influences were those of Nikolaus Harnoncourt and Franz Welser-Möst.'

'He always remains down to earth'

If Kaufmann felt at home in Zurich for as long as he did, this was due not least to colleagues such as Michael Volle, his baritone partner in *Fierrabras* and *La bohème*. Whenever the two of them met, there was always lots to laugh about, often to the dismay of the directors with whom they were working. And, of course, the urge to laugh is greatest when they were not supposed to do so – when another singer enters through the wrong door, for example, and the well-rehearsed scene is suddenly thrown into disarray.

'I know few singers as far removed from a diva's airs and graces as Jonas,' says Michael Volle, recalling, in part, their rehearsals together in London. 'He is far too grounded for that. And if he belts out a top C at a morning rehearsal, deafening you in the process, then this is simply an expression of his love of life. I wish we could appear together more often and perhaps perform duets together or record an album of duets. We recorded the scene between Tamino and the Speaker for his 2009 album of scenes from Mozart, Schubert, Beethoven and Wagner conducted by Claudio Abbado. It was a great pleasure for me to do so. It would be wonderful to do *Tosca* together. To send him off to the torture chamber would be quite something! What I particularly admire about him is his integrity and his honesty: towards the work, towards the audience, towards his colleagues – and towards himself.'

In German there is a saying, 'Dumm, dümmer, Tenor', meaning 'Dumb, dumber, tenor'. Vesselina Kasarova was no doubt alluding to this when she emphasized Kaufmann's intelligence, only to correct herself with a laugh: 'It's a wonderful combination of a great voice, musicality, intellect and a real ability to act. He's got everything he needs to reach the top of his profession and to remain there. I'm delighted that he has managed to get to the very top. How many singers with great abilities have fallen by the wayside because they didn't get the right break at the right time!'

It is usually a company's orchestral musicians and the members of its chorus who provide the best indication of the esteem in which a soloist is held. 'Even the women in the chorus cried' is the best compliment that a singer can receive in Berlin. There is a similar story in Zurich about the oboist Bernhard Heinrichs. The first time he heard Kaufmann as Florestan, he was a little sceptical: 'No, I thought, now he'll darken his tone as Domingo used to do as Otello, so baritonal, but that's not what he is. And with hindsight I have to say that I was wrong. That's precisely his sound. At the time I still had his Tamino in my mind's ear and in that role he sounded far brighter, of course. But his voice has developed and he can sing difficult and heavy parts like Florestan quite effortlessly. And the great thing is that in spite of this dark quality to his tone, his top notes still have a heroic gleam to them. In general his entire voice is very well focused, even when he is singing quietly. I had to leave the pit during a rehearsal for the Verdi *Requiem*, but I could still hear his *piano* singing even through the closed doors, so concentrated was the sound. As I was standing outside in the foyer, I couldn't help remembering what we oboists are taught: "Play a *piano* with an intensity that allows even the lavatory attendant to hear it." It's clear that some people treat him differently after his tremendous success at the Met. It's always like that when someone has made it big. But he himself hasn't changed at all in terms of his behaviour. Whether in rehearsal or in the canteen, he is always entirely natural, he always remains down to earth.'

Alexander Pereira: 'An out-and-out phenomenon'

Normally tenors are divided into different categories: there are some for the Italian and French repertory, some for Mozart, some for Wagner. But Jonas Kaufmann is a tenor for whom all of these categories are meaningless. I know of no singer who without further ado is capable of singing Bizet's Don José today and Puccini's Cavaradossi or Wagner's Parsifal tomorrow. But Jonas Kaufmann can do this. We're dealing here with an out-and-out phenomenon. His 'secret' seems to me to be his inner calm, the naturalness and composure which ensure that his voice can always resonate freely; that a voice which is in fact dark and almost baritonal can sing the high notes that are normally difficult to reach with this particular colour.

I should add that his debut at the Royal Opera in London came about thanks to a chance occurrence in my office. He was supposed to sing Bacchus in *Ariadne auf Naxos* for us in Zurich, but he was keen to do the first night of *Carmen* in London. Since we were unable to agree, I said: 'All right, we'll toss a coin!' Unfortunately I lost. But it's a small loss in view of all that he sang in Zurich. I think that the Zurich Opera offered him some great projects at the decisive moment and in that way contributed to the fact that his career took off with such explosive force. That makes me very happy.

'Do they really mean me?'

Met debut

It is early afternoon on Saturday, 4 February 2006. In his apartment on New York's Upper West Side, only a few minutes' walk from the Met, Jonas Kaufmann is preparing for his house debut with keep-fit exercises, yoga and autogenic training. Normally he lies down for an hour before the performance, but today his adrenalin level is too high. This, after all, is his debut in a house where every singer dreams of performing. He is singing Alfredo Germont in Verdi's *La traviata* in a production by Franco Zeffirelli.

Literally, 'La traviata' means 'the woman who has strayed'. The opera tells the well-known tale of the Lady of the Camellias, the hapless courtesan who succumbs to tuberculosis. Her historical model was Marie Duplessis, who in the middle of the nineteenth century was one of the principal attractions of Paris's demi-monde. In his autobiographical novel *La dame aux camélias* Alexandre Dumas *fils* raised a literary monument to *la grande horizontale*. In Dumas she is called Marguerite Gautier, in Verdi Violetta Valéry.

The role of Violetta is one of the most demanding in the whole of the soprano repertory, and many singers – even some famous ones – have foundered on its demands, especially those posed by the tricky coloratura writing in the virtuoso cabaletta 'Sempre libera' at the end of the opening act.

Tonight's prima donna is Angela Gheorghiu. The city's opera buffs have been awaiting her appearances with feverish impatience, for it was as Violetta that the beautiful Romanian soprano had made her international breakthrough at Covent Garden a decade earlier. Since then she has been one of the VIPs of the classical scene and has already sung over fifty performances at the Met, including Mimì in *La bohème* and Marguerite in *Faust*, but as yet she has not been heard as Violetta. She had found Zeffirelli's production too opulent, too lacking in intimacy and too old-fashioned. But the company's general manager, Joseph Volpe, had refused to give up and after endless discussions her resistance had finally crumbled. Before she agreed to appear, however, another matter needed to be clarified: who would be singing Alfredo? Volpe had his sights on a young German tenor. Gheorghiu was delighted, for she had seen his Lindoro on a DVD of Paisiello's *Nina* from Zurich and enjoyed it immensely.

The story of Kaufmann's Met debut had begun in the spring of 2001, when he had auditioned at the Philharmonie in Munich. In the front row was James Levine, the Met's long-standing principal conductor and artistic director. After the first aria he had climbed up onto the stage and sat down at the piano, asking Kaufmann: 'Do you mind if we do a little work together?' After they had spent some time on a number of passages from Tamino's Aria, Levine had said: 'Wonderful! We should think about what we can do together.'

Six months later – and eleven days after 9/11 – Kaufmann made his debut with the Lyric Opera of Chicago, singing Cassio in a production of *Otello* starring Ben Heppner and Renée Fleming. He flew to New York between the last two performances and again auditioned for Levine. He found himself standing alone on the stage of a house that seats 3,800, while Levine sat in the darkened auditorium. He sang arias from *Die Zauberflöte* and *La traviata*, and again Levine was much

Jonas Kaufmann, 1974.

(Jonas Kaufmann's archive)

In the kitchen with his
mother and sister, 1975.
(Jonas Kaufmann's archive)

Hiking with his father, 1976
(Jonas Kaufmann's archiv

With his sister,
Christmas 1978.

Kaufmann's first new production in Saarbrücken: *Carmen*, the Smugglers' Quintet with Althea-Maria Papoulias (Frasquita), Barbara Hahn (Carmen), Margarete Joswig (Mercédès), Jonas Kaufmann (Remendado) and Rupprecht Braun (Dancaïre), September 1994.

(Uwe Merkel – Staatstheater Saabrücken)

'Jonas Kaufmann outstanding as Tom' (*Frankfurter Allgemeine Zeitung*, 26 November 1996): a scene from the world premiere of Antonio Bibalo's *The Glass Menagerie* in Trier, with Helen Centner (Amanda) and Kirstin Hasselmann (Laura), 3 November 1996.

(Fotostudio Exklusiv Vera von Glasner GmbH – Theater Trier)

Rehearsing with Giorgio Strehler in Milan, 1997.
(Luigi Ciminaghi – Piccolo Teatro di Milano)

Kaufmann's United States debut as Cassio in Verdi's *Otello* at the Lyric Opera of Chicago, 22 September 2001.
(Robert Kusel – Lyric Opera of Chicago)

A chorus of boos: a scene from Stefan Herheim's production of Mozart's *Die Entführung aus dem Serail* at the 2003 Salzburg Festival, with Íride Martínez (Konstanze), Diana Damrau (Blondchen), Dietmar Kerschbaum (Pedrillo) and Kaufmann (Belmonte).

(Karl Forster – Salzburger Festspiele)

Kaufmann's Covent Garden debut as Ruggero opposite Angela Gheorghiu's Magda in Puccini's *La rondine*, 12 November 2004.

(Catherine Ashmore – Royal Opera House)

Debut at the Met: with Angela
Gheorghiu in *La traviata*,
4 February 2006.
(Ken Howard – Metropolitan Opera)

In the title role in Verdi's *Don Carlo* at
the Zurich Opera, November 2007.
(Suzanne Schwiertz – Opernhaus Zürich)

With Anna Netrebko in *La traviata* in London, January 2008.
(Catherine Ashmore – Royal Opera House)

With Daniel Barenboim and Plácido Domingo after the first night of
Carmen at La Scala, Milan, 7 December 2009.

(Marco Brescia – Teatro alla Scala)

As Cavaradossi in Luc Bondy's *Tosca*, a co-production between the Met,
the Bavarian State Opera and La Scala, Milan, 2010.

(Wilfried Hösl – Bayerische Staatsoper)

With Annette Dasch (Elsa) in Hans Neuenfels's
Lohengrin production, Bayreuth Festival, 2010.

As Siegmund in Robert Lepage's Met production of the *Ring*, seen here with
Eva-Maria Westbroek (Sieglinde) in a scene from *Die Walküre*, April 2011.

taken with what he had heard, even considering the prospect of his house debut. Elated, Kaufmann attended that evening's performance at the Met: *La bohème* with Ramón Vargas. He returned the following evening, this time for *Idomeneo* with Plácido Domingo.

Four and a half years were to pass before he himself returned to the stage of the Met and saw the vast auditorium again. All of the rehearsals for *La traviata* had taken place on a rehearsal stage in a dusty, badly ventilated hall. At no point was he offered a stage-and-orchestra rehearsal on the main stage.

Only when the prelude ended and the curtain rose on 4 February 2006 did Kaufmann know what it feels like to perform with an orchestra in a sold-out Metropolitan Opera. He had already made himself swear that he would not be distracted by the size of the auditorium but would concentrate on his role and on his partners. And there were numerous details that he had to keep in mind on his entrance: where are the steps? To whom do I give my hat, coat and gloves? Whom do I greet first? When do I go over to Violetta? And so on.

When Alfredo sets foot on the stage, the party in Violetta's salon is already in full swing, the atmosphere one of high spirits. It is Alfredo who launches the first of the opera's musical highlights, the famous Brindisi, or drinking song. Everything was running smoothly.

Then comes the moment when all of the guests withdraw. Alfredo hides in his hostess's salon with the intention of speaking to her on her own. Since this was the first time that Kaufmann had worked on the actual set, he failed to notice a wall lamp and struck his head against it. The noise was audible even in the back row of the Family Circle. The audience laughed.

With any other singer this might have made them more nervous, but for Kaufmann it had the effect of liberating him.

Bumping his head against the lamp released all the tension in his body and he could now breathe freely at last.

In the next scene Alfredo tells the beautiful Violetta that he loves her. By now Kaufmann was completely consumed by his role. At the same time he could sense that the audience, too, was being drawn into the action – it was one of those moments that arise when the chemistry between the performers really works.

As he is leaving, Violetta gives Alfredo a camellia: 'Bring it back when it's withered!' – 'Oh God! Tomorrow?' – 'Very well, tomorrow!'

Left alone in her salon, Violetta broods on their encounter. Could this be the great love of her life? No, such thoughts are foolish, delusional. She is fated to remain free and independent and to enjoy her life to the full – and who knows how long she will be able to do so. The ensuing cabaletta, 'Sempre libera', is an impassioned hymn to freedom and pleasure. Angela Gheorghiu does not sing it as a virtuoso showpiece but allows the audience to sense the extent to which Violetta is repressing her true feelings. She rejoices at something in which she no longer believes. Offstage we hear Alfredo's voice: 'Amor, amor è palpito dell'universo intero' ('Love is the pulse of the whole world'). The voice of the man she loves is at the same time the voice of her own palpitating heart. Violetta feels momentarily faint, then repeats 'Sempre libera' with even greater intensity. This is the moment when the soprano must reveal her true colours. Angela Gheorghiu gives it her all. The audience goes wild.

Act Two opens with the tenor's only monologue, a lyrical aria with an ebullient cabaletta ending on a high C. Verdi didn't write this note, but it is now a matter of honour for all tenors to sing it, at least to the extent that the conductor does not refuse to allow them to interpolate it at the very end. Listeners expect it, and some members of the audience even wait in the expectation that something will go wrong. This evening's conductor, Marco Armiliato, is no purist and allows Kaufmann a free hand. More importantly, he breathes with the singers, smiling at them and sharing their delight when a phrase goes especially well. For Kaufmann, this is a huge support, not least on this particular evening. Feeling confident, he sings his aria, 'De' miei bollenti spiriti', with heartfelt sensibility in exactly the way that his role as a young lover requires. The cabaletta then allows him to demonstrate the depth of passion that is to be found in the character of Alfredo. Only in the case of the final top C is Kaufmann unable to remain entirely relaxed, and so he plays it safe. The note is in place, but he feels that it could have been freer. A handful of music lovers may have noticed this detail, but to judge by the applause the audience's enthusiasm is not in doubt.

The rest of Act Two belongs to Gheorghiu and to the baritone Anthony Michaels-Moore in the role of Alfredo's father. In the great scene that unfolds between them the love story takes a tragic turn: in order not to compromise the honour and reputation of the Germont family, Violetta promises to end her relationship with Alfredo.

Meanwhile Kaufmann waits in his dressing room, trying to remain in character and to avoid thinking about who he is and what he is doing here. He knows that he was already successful in Chicago in the same role. But who in New York knows this, apart from a few opera buffs? For most members of the Met audience he is an unknown, a German tenor in the Italian repertory singing a role that has previously been the preserve of 'Italian' tenors – even if they hail from Spain or Mexico. Admittedly, the lines separating Verdi and Puccini on the one hand and Wagner and Strauss on the other have become blurred in the wake of the internationalization of opera, but it is still unusual for a German tenor to appear in *La traviata*. Of course, Kaufmann assumes that he is not the focus of interest. People have come to hear Angela Gheorghiu, and it is probably a matter of indifference to most of the audience whether the tenor is called Müller or Molinari.

'Mr Kaufmann, please!' a voice announces over the backstage intercom. He has to return to the stage for the final scene in Act Two, in which Alfredo learns the bitter truth: Violetta has written a letter breaking off their relationship and bidding him farewell.

During the interval, Kaufmann bumps into Victor Callegari, the Met's long-standing dresser, in the corridor outside his dressing room. Callegari heard the legendary Franco Corelli, the gladiator among tenors, and recalls the 'battle of the giants' in *Turandot*: Corelli's partner was Birgit Nilsson, who could produce a bigger sound than any other soprano at that time. The Riddle Scene had been sung according to the motto: 'Anything you can do, I can do louder.'

Kaufmann laughs out loud. 'You've a sunny disposition,' a colleague expresses his surprise. 'You're making your debut and talking and laughing?' But for Kaufmann laughter is the best thing he can do in moments like these. It relaxes his body and ensures the continuing flexibility of the muscles which support the tone. As a result, he is fairly composed for his next scene, which also happens to be his favourite. Here he can display his whole stage temperament when exposing Violetta before the assembled menfolk and throwing in her face the money that he has won at the gaming tables. Portraying a character onstage is a form of therapy for him: he can release feelings of aggression and live out emotions which might be destructive in real life. The audience senses this: they are watching a singer who is not just plying his trade as an actor but throwing himself into the part body and soul.

Act Four: Violetta is dying. Too late she receives a letter from Giorgio Germont explaining the reasons for his actions. But there is still time for a final meeting with Alfredo. He knows that there is no longer any hope for her but does not want to rob her of the illusion and so he paints the picture of a happy future together: you'll get better and you'll be the light of my life, he tells her. 'We'll leave Paris, my dearest.' He sings these lines to Violetta alone. He wants to give her something to hold on to. It is a moment of the greatest tenderness and the deepest despair. While singing it, Kaufmann remembers something that Margarete Joswig said to him after his first *La traviata* in Stuttgart: 'You can do this completely differently. Sing as softly and as tenderly as you possibly can.' Fortunately, the Met is a house where this will work: even the quietest note will carry to the very back row, assuming that the singer has the ability to project his or her tone.

He succeeds in doing so. Angela Gheorghiu and Marco Armiliato take up the same tender, intimate tone, and the audience reacts in the same vein. The audience's coughs had previously been so disruptive that Jay Nordlinger, writing in the *New York Sun*, had half expected the soprano to stop singing and say: 'Hey! I'm the one dying here!' But now you can hear a pin drop. A familiar operatic melody has suddenly become a moment of utter magic.

Afterwards a few listeners were heard saying that only now did they understand what 'Parigi, o cara' really meant and that they had been moved to tears by the hopelessness and fragile tenderness of this dreamlike vision.

Violetta dies in her lover's arms, and the curtain falls.

What happened next is one of the happiest moments in Jonas Kaufmann's life. 'First the whole cast took a bow, then came the individual curtain calls. Angela Gheorghiu was showered with shouts of "bravo". Before it was my turn, I thought: "Well, I guess they'll clap politely." I came out – and people jumped up from their seats and shouted! I simply couldn't understand it, it literally bowled me over. I know only that I went weak at the knees and thought: do they really mean me? It sounds just like the cliché familiar from the Oscars, but that's exactly how I felt at that moment – simply because I'd never reckoned on a reaction like that. After all, I'd sung the part of Alfredo a few times before that, in Stuttgart and Chicago, and people had thought it very nice. But for an entire house to go wild with excitement and for people who don't know me to shout "bravo" – initially I couldn't grasp it at all. It was an unforgettable moment! Even today I get goosebumps just thinking about it.'

After the final curtain call, everyone onstage gathered around Kaufmann, congratulating him and shaking his hand: Joseph Volpe, his agents Bruce Zemsky and Alan Green, and his friends. All were there apart from his wife, who only a few weeks earlier had given birth to their third child and reluctantly had to remain at home. It would be a week later until she would hear her husband, when the next performance was broadcast all around the world on the radio.

Immediately after the performance Margarete received a fax from one of her friends: 'Jonas came out – and a sold-out house stood up and bellowed "bravo". Tears came to my eyes. He sang and acted so magnificently that in the dressing room they were saying "A star is born". You'd have been proud!'

And Verdi too – at least according to the *New York Sun*. Elsewhere, the famous music critic Peter G. Davis compared Kaufmann and Gheorghiu to Hollywood's dream couple of Brad Pitt and Angelina Jolie: 'Brangelina sings' was the headline in the *New York Magazine*. 'Angela Gheorghiu and Jonas Kaufmann do as much for the eyes as for the ears. [...] Jonas Kaufmann not only has the looks and easy stage bearing of a rock star, but he also has a flexibility seldom heard in German tenors – he sings Parsifal and Florestan with distinction, as well as lyrical roles like Alfredo. If his voice lacks the ringing lift up top that one ideally likes in a Verdi tenor, the overall tone is smoothly burnished, beautifully focused on the notes, and always disarmingly musical.'

The telephone rarely stopped ringing and Kaufmann was showered with compliments and offers. He had made it.

Die Walküre *and 'the machine'*

With these performances of *La traviata*, Kaufmann became a star overnight, Peter Gelb – general manager of the Met since August 2006 – later recalled, before going on to describe the tenor as being in a class of his own. If comparisons were to be drawn with any other tenor, it would be with Plácido Domingo: both men commanded an unusually broad repertory, allowing Kaufmann to be heard at the Met in roles as varied as Verdi and Mozart, Bizet and Puccini, Wagner and Massenet.

Because opera houses and concert halls have to plan so far ahead – in the case of international houses, this may be as much as five years – it took a while for Kaufmann to demonstrate his versatility at the Met. After his appearances as Alfredo in *La traviata* in February 2006, he returned in October of the same year for three performances of *Die Zauberflöte*; revivals of *La traviata* followed in March 2007 and March 2008; in 2007 it was Krassimira Stoyanova who sang Violetta, while Ruth Ann Swenson took over the following year. According to Peter Gelb, the two years' silence that ensued was due to an endless series of commitments in Europe and was a source of much annoyance to listeners in New York who would have liked to hear much more of him.

Kaufmann's 'comeback' in a new production of *Tosca* in April 2010 proved a triumph. With Patricia Racette in the title role, Bryn Terfel as Scarpia and Fabio Luisi on the podium, the musical aspect of the performance helped the audience to come to terms with Luc Bondy's visually unappealing production, subsequently seen in Munich and Milan. Spontaneous applause greeted Kaufmann's sustained top notes in 'Vittoria! Vittoria!', and after 'E lucevan le stelle' the shouts of 'bravo' went on for several minutes. A few days later he appeared in two repertory performances of *Carmen*.

In 2011, however, New Yorkers could no longer complain, as Kaufmann was involved in two new productions – *Die Walküre* and *Faust* – and gave a song recital at the Met, while also taking part in a concert performance of *Adriana Lecouvreur* at Carnegie Hall and appearing at the Richard Tucker Gala that Barry Tucker organizes every year in memory of his father. It was an extremely successful series of performances, even if it got off to a difficult start, when the rehearsals for *Die Walküre* – the second part of the Met's new production of the *Ring* – ran into various problems. James Levine was suffering from acute back pain, and Robert Lepage, the director of numerous films and stage plays such as *Lipsynch* and *The Anderson Project*, but with little experience in opera, devoted most of his time and energy to his lavishly expensive, computer-generated sets. The singers were quite literally dwarfed by their massive structure. 'The relationships between the characters are far from clear,' *Die Welt* wrote after the first night, 'they are all just chess pieces caught up in a vast and hugely expensive motor known simply as "the machine". Weighing forty-five tons, it comprises twenty-four swivelling beams which move up and down and can be used as a video screen, while also turning into a flight of steps, opening up to reveal a surface for projections and serving as a rocking horse and a slide for the Ride of the Valkyries.' According to the *New York Times*, Lepage had been so intent on showing what his monumental toy could do that he even banished Brünnhilde to the wings during the most powerful moment in her role. When the production was later relayed to cinemas all over the world in high definition and edited for DVD, the singers finally came into their own: thanks to the use of close-ups and Gary Halvorson's television direction, Kaufmann and his fellow performers – Deborah Voigt

(Brünnhilde), Eva-Maria Westbroek (Sieglinde) and Bryn Terfel (Wotan) – were able to assert their presence by means of their acting, gestures and facial expressions. The machine appeared less dominant than it had been when seen from the auditorium during the live performances.

How did you cope with this structure?
For me it wasn't that great, especially in light of the expense that it involved. And it kept going wrong. We simply didn't trust it. If you were walking on top of the beams, you could never be sure if they'd support you or not. This really doesn't inspire you to give your best: I think that singers should have other things on their mind than worrying about their own safety. There were lots of minor accidents and a couple of major ones that should have never been allowed to happen in the theatre. But as a result of all these stories, the press never stopped talking about the machine – which is in itself a kind of PR. I'm only afraid that because it was so technically lavish, this *Ring* won't have much of a future, and that is a pity. This is something that I see not only at the Met, but elsewhere, too: works which are so powerful that it should be possible to perform them frequently are unfortunately staged as if they were exceptional pieces that have to be taken out of the repertory after only a couple of seasons because they are too specialized for a large audience. But operas like *Tosca* and *Die Walküre* should be able to remain in the repertory without the need for increased expense once the original cast has been replaced.

Like Boleslaw Barlog's production of Tosca *at the Deutsche Oper in Berlin. It could still be performed twenty or thirty years after it had first been seen, without people having to feel ashamed about it.*
With Puccini's operas the music already indicates how the action should be staged, so you really can't turn these works upside

down. If you still insist on doing so, the energy of the piece is inevitably reduced. It's like driving a Porsche in your backyard. And that's the problem with many directors. They're afraid of the energy of the music. Or at the very least they mistrust this energy.

Because of state subsidies, European houses can risk production disasters more than American companies.
Of course. The Met can't afford to do what Klaus Zehelein did in Stuttgart, which was to bring in an entirely new audience by getting rid of the old one. The Met is a house financed exclusively by box-office income and private sponsorship. Although I wasn't happy with the productions of *Tosca* and *Die Walküre*, the Met's general manager, Peter Gelb, knows what's needed to run his house successfully. He wanted to break free from the design-led productions more reminiscent of a revue and offer his audiences modern interpretations – 'modern' by American standards: stylish and unusual, but not insane. He has brought off this balancing act, and his successes prove that he was right.

Back to Die Walküre *at the Met: it was a role debut under difficult conditions. Did this affect your self-confidence?*
Not in so many words, but there were times when I was naturally worried. To sing a role like Siegmund for the first time at the Met isn't entirely without its risks. But in cases like that you concentrate more on the technical demands of the role. Only when you sing the part for a second or a third time can you devote yourself to interpretative details. So I was all the more delighted at the acclaim. People jumped up from their seats and shouted as if I'd sung a pop song. It wasn't the sort of reaction one expects in Wagner, certainly not after the opening act. I was again reminded of the great moment following my Met debut. And I was no more prepared for it after *Die Walküre* than I had been after *La traviata* in 2006.

Wasn't it also risky to sing Faust at the Met after Siegmund? Normally singers perform lyric roles before moving on to a more dramatic repertory.

I don't see any danger in this. Quite the opposite, in fact. I think it's much healthier from a vocal point of view to mix lyric and dramatic parts instead of singing only heavy parts after Siegmund. If I were to do so, I'd inevitably find that one day my voice wasn't flexible enough to cope with the subtler shades of a role like Faust or Don Carlo.

Song recital at the Met

For you, the evening of 30 October 2011 must have placed you under an even bigger spotlight than the first night of Faust. *Your song recital was the first solo recital in the house since Luciano Pavarotti's in 1994. Isn't singing lieder at the Met like looking through the wrong end of a telescope?*

It's true that from a purely optical standpoint you don't have the same sort of communication with the whole audience as you do in a chamber music room. But it works well acoustically. In the first place, the auditorium at the Met is relatively round, so the distance between you and the back row isn't as great as it is in rectangular houses like the Alte Oper in Frankfurt. And, second, the acoustics are really very good. I knew from my operatic performances that a singer's most delicate *piano* carries to the back row, so to that extent I wasn't afraid that up to half of the subtleties in my interpretation could be lost.

So you didn't opt for a special programme just for the Met but performed the one you'd already sung in smaller venues: Mahler, Liszt, Duparc and Strauss.

Exactly. I don't think it's a good idea to present a programme tailored entirely to the size of a house. If the space doesn't lend itself to certain songs, then it is in general not suitable for lieder and in that case you should avoid it. And to sing only 'war-horses' at the Met would be as pointless as to spend two and a half hours just crooning in a smaller house. Song recitals draw their strength from their use of contrast.

How can you fill such a large hall if you sing quietly?
The keywords are 'projection' and 'confidence' – in other words, the confidence that your voice will carry in such a large space just as well as it does in a smaller one. The biggest mistake that you could make would be to think that the bigger the house, the more voice you need. That's completely un-necessary at the Met. I was surprised to discover that it's just as possible to sing quietly and create an intimate atmosphere in this space as it is elsewhere. It's the same in the Teatro Colón in Buenos Aires, where I had the pleasure of singing a concert and a recital during my South American debut tour in August 2016.

In 2013 you were the protagonist in a new Parsifal, *in 2014 you sang the title role in a new* Werther. *Your last performance was on 15 March 2014. Since then the Met audience has been waiting for your return.*
We had planned a series of performances of *Manon Lescaut* in February 2016, but unfortunately I had to cancel due to ill-ness. After that Peter Gelb offered me the new production of *Tosca*, which is to have its premiere on New Year's Eve 2017. But I decided to make some changes in my schedule and avoid exceedingly long periods away from home. And since the Met isn't exactly a short-distance flight away I had to ask for a reduced rehearsal period and in consequence fewer perform-ances. But for the *Tosca* the Met wanted all or nothing, so they got nothing. I'm very sorry about it, but I'm sure we will find a more satisfying solution next time.

Many artists say that they enjoy spending a month or two in New York but that they couldn't live there because their senses are permanently overstimulated.

I can understand that, but for my own part I find all these stimuli a huge draw. The fact that you need a vast amount of energy to be able to live there is something I notice only when I'm back at home.

Musicals

What do you do in New York when you're not singing or aren't invited out?

Whenever I have the time, I attend other performances, either at the Met or on Broadway. I like to watch musicals, partly to see how the entertainment industry functions and partly to see how these productions are done. You can learn a lot from them. I went to see *The Book of Mormon*, for example, and laughed till I cried. Say what you like about the dirty jokes, but it's a great show. I feel more drawn towards the classical musicals, which lie at the interface between operetta and pop. Take Gershwin's *Anything Goes*, for example. It's simply highly professional, first-class entertainment. And when judged by European standards, it's insane to see how much money they take in and what the turnover is. If even half of this were invested in good operetta productions in Europe, we'd undoubtedly be just as successful. I think it's really regrettable that operetta is so neglected today, even though it often has the better music. Instead of intellectualizing operetta, people should try to use the pull of the music to tell a good and racy story. That should really work!

Have you ever been offered a role in a musical?
In his last season at the Vienna State Opera Ioan Holender wanted to do *West Side Story* with Anna Netrebko and me, but in the end the idea came to nothing. I have to say that I didn't take the offer entirely seriously, but today I guess I know what he wanted.

High Definition: opera in the cinema

So far you've appeared in four productions at the Met which have been broadcast to cinemas all over the world and later released on DVD: Die Walküre, Faust, Parsifal and Werther. What does it feel like to know that this afternoon it won't be 3,800 people watching you but several million?
In fact it's really no different from normal. It makes no difference whether it's several thousand or several million if you're sure of your voice and your interpretation of a role. I've often been asked if I'd approach a part differently knowing that microphones and cameras were present, but the answer is no. If you feel what you're singing, then the *pianissimo* notes and the little gestures will carry to the very back row. And a portrayal that stems from genuine emotion will appear credible both in close-ups and from a distance. But if you don't feel something with your heart and soul and if you perform it only mechanically, then the audience will find it artificial. In a word: if your expression is right, then your body language and posture will also be right.

On the subject of close-ups, Elisabeth Schwarzkopf has argued that the art of singing presupposes illusion and distance and that this sense of illusion is destroyed if the camera peers down the performer's throat and shows their fillings and tonsils. For Schwarzkopf, this is a form of pornography.
Extreme close-ups can be disillusioning because you don't always present your most attractive face to the world when

singing. On the other hand, some viewers think that it's a good thing to see the effort that goes into singing and to know that it doesn't just fall into the singer's lap. An opera like *Parsifal* that lasts five hours is already a strain if you know that you are being watched all the time – above all because there are long stretches when Parsifal doesn't sing at all but stands onstage as a silent witness. In spite of this, you can't stop concentrating even for a moment. You have to stay in character every second of the performance.

What in general is your opinion of cinema relays of operas?
To be honest, I was initially sceptical. With television broadcasts of operas I was always disturbed by the fact that the television director decides what I'm allowed to see, with the result that many details can get lost. Especially with operas that I know well, I got really worked up. But cinema broadcasts from the Met are incredibly skilfully done. Even the camera movements are sheer poetry. It's like a feature film produced over umpteen days of filming. And yet it's live! It's on an unbelievably high level. So I can understand why it fascinates even theatregoers and is always so successful. Assuming this degree of excellence, cinema broadcasts of operas can achieve something that we all dream of by winning over audiences for whom a visit to the opera is too expensive or too elitist or who don't go to the opera because they think it needs advance preparation and insider knowledge. To that extent cinema broadcasts can achieve the same degree of democratization as CDs and DVDs, the decisive difference being that they're live and you can share your experience with others. At the same time, you're far closer to the action onstage than if you're sitting in the auditorium. You can see the faces, the expressions, the actions and reactions much more clearly. And if the quality of the relay is as good as it is with high-definition broadcasts from the Met, then the result is outstanding.

Management and PR

Dumbing down

Talk of a crisis in the classical music industry now seems to be an inescapable cliché, and yet everyone working in the classical music business is heartily sick of the complaints about the drop in sales figures and the prognostications of the end of the educated middle classes. 'Audiences are made up entirely of old people' is the lament that for years has been endlessly repeated. This sounds like too much of a generalization, and indeed it is. Even so, the trend is undeniable: for a long time classical music has no longer occupied the position in our lives that it did forty or fifty years ago, when music was a compulsory subject in schools in the same way that English and maths were an obligatory part of the curriculum; blue- and white-collar workers went to the theatre on a regular basis; and there was singing and music-making in many households. People would also meet to listen to records and to radio broadcasts together.

With the advent of the CD the classical music industry enjoyed a new lease of life between 1985 and 1995. In 1990 Klaus Umbach, music journalist at *Der Spiegel*, wrote a maliciously witty piece entitled 'Geldschein-Sonate', an allusion to Beethoven's 'Mondschein' ('Moonlight') Sonata, but with the moonlight replaced by banknotes. In it he was able to make fun of some of the grotesque scenes that were currently unfolding in a world of classical music gambling with its own future. Once the CD boom was over, the great decline began, bringing with it desperate attempts to popularize classical music. More often than not the baby was thrown out with the bathwater: record companies were 'restructured' out of existence, municipal theatres subjected to swingeing cuts, public broadcasters reformed to the point where they were no longer recognizable and the greatest works of classical music were reduced to pleasant tunes. Developments long familiar from the pop industry were now transferred to the classical music business, policy being dictated by viewing figures and by an attitude that can only be described as dumbing down. This was the heyday of questionable projects and products that included Lolita-like violinists in wet T-shirts, playgirls with a cello clasped between their legs and artists who, aware of their limited resources, preferred to mime to a pre-recorded tape rather than risk performing live. 'Crossover' was the magic formula – at least until it became a term of abuse in the industry. Meanwhile ignorance had a field day as managerial posts at record companies were filled with pop managers with no experience of the classical market, with the result that many a conversation between an artist and a company's managing director turned out to be unprofessional and even embarrassing. Among insiders, wonderful anecdotes circulated about tragi-comical clashes at press conferences and bizarre congratulations backstage.

Perfect timing

This phase now seems to belong to the past – or at least the classical music industry hopes as much. After all, hasn't the old-fashioned view prevailed, namely, that quality endures? Is the media presence of artists such as Plácido Domingo, Daniel

Barenboim, Cecilia Bartoli and Anna Netrebko not proof that content is at least as important as packaging? Is the PR hype with which record companies tried to turn mediocre artists into world-class talents not long since *passé*? Who speaks nowadays of all the 'shooting stars' with which these companies sought to make a quick profit twenty years ago?

Jonas Kaufmann's rise to the top league of singers began at the very time when what were thought to be solutions to classical music's problems were finally being seen as aberrations. From a superficial standpoint, this was a stroke of luck, granting the tenor the sort of benefits that are often enjoyed by latecomers. In fact Kaufmann owed his success to a combination of intelligence and instinct coupled with perfect timing. He demonstrated intelligence in terms of his choice of roles and his assessment of his own vocal development. He showed a good instinct with regard to management and marketing. And he revealed perfect timing to the extent that in general he met the right people at the right time: his teacher Michael Rhodes, artistic directors like Alexander Pereira, great artists like Giorgio Strehler and Antonio Pappano and responsible managers like Bruce Zemsky and Alan Green. Moreover, he had often seen how the industry's 'shooting stars' had plummeted back to earth with the same speed with which they had first been catapulted skywards. Kaufmann knew exactly what he wanted: not a meteoric career but a continuous development. Take Chicago, for example: most singers would have leapt at the chance to make their Lyric Opera debut in a leading role. Not so Kaufmann, who instead of Alfredo in *La traviata* chose the small role of Cassio in *Otello*. Karajan, who divided singers into cats and dogs, would have placed him in the former group: 'When you say to a dog: "Jump!", it jumps,' the conductor had explained to Christa Ludwig after she had turned down his offer to sing Isolde and Brünnhilde. 'But if you say this to a cat, it doesn't jump until it's certain that it can really manage the manoeuvre.'

It is this same caution that prevented Jonas Kaufmann from taking any risks following his vocal crisis in Saarbrücken. 'In all the years that I've known him,' says Christian Lange, who managed the tenor during his early career and who continues to organize some of his recitals, 'I've never known him take on a challenge that completely overtaxed him. His timing was always perfect and he knows exactly what is good for his voice and his body and what isn't.'

Zemsky and Green

Since 2008 Kaufmann has been represented internationally by Zemsky/Green Artists Management of New York. 'I'd previously been looked after by various managers in Europe and the United States, which became problematic in time since they all wanted a share of the cake. Conflicts were almost inevitable. And so I decided that from the end of 2007 I'd be represented by only one agency worldwide. Bruce Zemsky and Alan Green had previously advised me well, often to their own financial disadvantage, and that had impressed me a lot.'

Where opera and classical music were concerned, Alan Green had a natural advantage. His mother was born Beatrice Waghalter in Berlin in 1913. Married three times, she was, according to an obituary that appeared in the Berlin daily *Der Tagesspiegel* in 2001, a 'singer at the wrong time', while his grandfather Ignatz Waghalter (1881–1949) was a composer and the first principal conductor in the history of the Deutsche Oper in Berlin. In 1912, when the new theatre opened in Charlottenburg with Beethoven's *Fidelio*, it was still called the Deutsches Opernhaus. Waghalter conducted several first nights there between 1912 and 1923, including the local premiere of Puccini's *La fanciulla del West* in the presence of the composer, and the world premieres of three of his own operas. For the 1924–5 season he was appointed Joseph Stransky's successor as music director of the New York Philharmonic, but he remained there for only a season, his longing for Germany proving greater than any desire to become a permanent feature of New York's musical life. The racism of the National Socialists destroyed his life in Germany and in 1934 he fled to Austria, later escaping with his family to the United States only a few weeks before Austria was annexed by Germany in 1938. For his daughter, too, emigration meant a downturn in her career. Once hailed by Fritzi Massary as her natural successor, Beatrice Waghalter had to start afresh in New York. Even so, she was able to appear on the radio, singing for half an hour a week as the 'Viennese Nightingale'. In 1954 she married a successful businessman, Russell Green. Alan Green is their son.

Alan Green's first memory of the Met is a performance of *Die Meistersinger von Nürnberg* in 1964 with Paul Schöffler, Ingrid Bjoner and Jess Thomas. When I listed the names of the rest of the cast, he shook his head and sighed: 'How can you know that? You're as sick as I am.' The German tenor Peter Seiffert once said something similar about his early appearances in the children's chorus at the Deutsche Oper am Rhein: 'From then on I was an addict – an opera addict.' Whether sick or mad or simply passionate about music, young opera buffs have a hard time with things at school – but a comparatively easy time backstage. 'This is my grandson,' Richard Tucker's wife Sarah claimed while leading the young Bruce Zemsky past the stage door at the Met. The Tuckers used to cultivate the friendship of the standees, inviting them to their home.

Bruce Zemsky, who sadly passed away in August 2017, also hailed from New York. Both men were born in the same year and probably spent most of their school years in the standing room at the Met and listening to records. Zemsky attended the High School of Music and Art in New York City, where he displayed various talents, including writing some wonderful pop songs which have been performed with great success.

'Although music was my life,' he said, 'I was realistic and knew that I had to study something else in college.' So he enrolled at Queens College where he got his degree in Italian and minored in French. But opera remained his passion. His first full season as a standee at the Met was 1972–3, when he heard many great performances. The one that most stood out was hearing a performance of *Don Carlo* with an all-star cast: Franco Corelli, Montserrat Caballé, Grace Bumbry, Robert Merrill and Cesare Siepi. 'I was hooked forever and also spoiled as you don't hear a cast like that every day.' As former standees both Zemsky and Green soon learnt all about the opera industry, by no means a negligible advantage when it came to pursuing their later careers in artist management. In 2005 they formed their own company as Zemsky/Green Artists Management. Among the singers on their roster are Pretty Yende, Eva-Maria Westbroek, Ramón Vargas, Anita Rachvelishvili, Yonghoon Lee, Charles Castronovo and Ermonela Jaho.

Zemsky recalled meeting Jonas Kaufmann for the first time in December 2000. He was managing the soprano Cristina Gallardo-Domâs, who was recording a solo album with the Munich Radio Orchestra in the main studio at Bavarian Radio. 'A few days before they were to record Violetta's scene in the first act of *La traviata*, I was in the studio and asked the producer if they had a tenor to record Alfredo's few lines. He said not and that they planned on doing it without a tenor. "It's not very classy to have no tenor," I said. "Please get one." He agreed but forgot to engage one until the very morning of the session. Then they called Jonas on his mobile: he was out Christmas shopping but said he could come over and do it. I heard him sing two lines from the control room and thought, "Who is *that*?" When he was leaving the building, I wondered if I could leave Mrs Gallardo-Domâs alone for a minute and go to speak to Jonas. And I thought, "For a tenor like that, yes!" '

'Romantic Arias'

Kaufmann's first solo album was released in 2006 and was devoted to songs by Richard Strauss. His accompanist was Helmut Deutsch. When Zemsky and Green asked if they could speak to the managers of the French record company that had released it, they were told that the firm was not interested in making any more records with Kaufmann. Shortly after his Met debut, they met Bogdan Roščić, who was then the managing director of Decca Records in London and who became president of Sony Classical in New York in 2009.

'I first heard Jonas in the allegedly scandalous production of *Die Entführung* in Salzburg,' Roščić begins his Kaufmann reminiscences, 'and unlike many other people in the audience I thought that Stefan Herheim's reading was magnificent. It was a screwball comedy, witty and fast-moving, and Jonas was at the heart of it. My attempts to make contact with him were initially thwarted by a woman who was then a part of his management team. She claimed that he had other plans. I later discovered that my question never reached him. So it took a while for us to get together, and it was only when he was managed by Zemsky and Green that we arranged to meet following Jonas's debut at the Vienna State Opera. It was a repertory performance of *Die Zauberflöte*, as depressing as you can find only in a major house. Even from seventeen rows back you could see the holes in the material that had once covered the serpent. But I knew right away that I wanted to sign a contract with him at all costs. The only question that evening was agreeing on the basis for our work together. For his debut album we decided on a popular recital that finally appeared under the title *Romantic Arias*. I still remember hearing the first edits in my office; it was a great moment. For whatever great performances a singer may have given in the past, what interests CD buyers is only what comes out of their loudspeakers. At that time there was nothing else like it on the market. *Romantic Arias* hit the bull's eye in every way. It was undoubtedly the most powerful debut by a core classical artist for many years.'

For Roščić the Latin-lover look on the front cover of the CD was a welcome bonus: attractive packaging for attractive content. 'He looks great, but at the same time he is the perfect proof of the fact that on its own this is not enough. There are heaps of good-looking people who want to be stars but very few who have what it takes to enjoy an international career.'

Kaufmann had already made a number of recordings even before his album of Strauss lieder – they include complete recordings of Weber's *Oberon* under Sir John Eliot Gardiner and of Humperdinck's *Königskinder* under Armin Jordan – but *Romantic Arias* marked the start of his recording career as surely as his Met debut had done for his stage career. Since then he has recorded eleven solo albums and twenty-six complete operas, including two versions of *Tosca*, *Die Walküre* and *Carmen*. Millions of cinema-goers have seen him in Met broadcasts of *Die Walküre*, *Faust*, *Parsifal* and *Werther* as well as in London productions of *Manon Lescaut* and *Andrea Chénier*. Ever since his Munich *Lohengrin*, there have been few operatic productions with Kaufmann that have not been broadcast on the radio or recorded on video.

Most of Kaufmann's solo albums remained in the German classical music charts for weeks after their initial release: *Du bist die Welt für mich*, featuring tenor hits associated with Richard Tauber and the early sound-film era, even reached number eleven in the pop charts ahead of Lady Gaga. Should this then be a reason to market him according to the criteria and management strategies found in the world of pop music?

For Per Hauber, Sony Classical's senior vice-president since 2011, the situation is simple: 'Positioning Jonas Kaufmann could not be more straightforward. He is *the* tenor, and everyone is fighting over him. You don't need to push him or drown him in hype but simply have to weigh everything up carefully. When should he appear on television shows, for example? And which ones? Here audience figures are by no means the primary consideration. In the first place there are no longer any programmes on German-language television where you can be guaranteed a good return on your investment. In its heyday one such programme would have been the long-running game show *Wetten, dass?*, but this ended in 2014. Second, our experience indicates that it is better to choose programmes actually watched by an interested audience rather than prime-time shows with huge audience figures, where most households simply have the programme playing in the background. And, third, Jonas Kaufmann is one of the most popular singers of our day. He has appeared with Anna Netrebko at the open-air Waldbühne in Berlin, together with David Garrett he opened the Champions League final in the Allianz Arena in Munich, he has appeared with Lang Lang on the Bambi Show and can be seen in a feature film alongside John Malkovich. What more can you want?'

'He knows exactly what he wants and what he doesn't want,' Roščić adds, 'which is another reason why working with him is such a pleasure. He feels a degree of scepticism towards the classical music industry, including its rules and blandishments, that has nothing to do with vanity. Built into him is something like an unerring compass needle that ensures that he always has a sensible goal in his sights. He has no time for the sort of arbitrariness that we've experienced with other artists whose motto seems to be: "Whether it's Tchaikovsky or Brahms, the main thing is that we're in on it!" And I think that his supreme goal is precisely what I myself want for him above all else: to remain on the incredibly high artistic level that he has now reached. I also hope that he is better protected against the unreasonable expectations of the opera industry, especially mediocrities from the world of *Regietheater* who under the pretence of fomenting a scandal claim to be "relevant" but who in actual fact are hopelessly average. And, third, I wish him more time – in the first instance for himself, but also to enable him to deal with the backlog of decisions that inevitably has to be sorted out by an artist of his stature but which is often as hard to reduce as the European Union's butter mountain: as soon as one series of decisions has been taken, another immediately presents itself.'

This is a recurrent problem in Jonas Kaufmann's life and one that I myself have had to contend with on a daily basis ever since I started working for him. Even the requests for interviews and for promotional updates can snowball until they turn into a gigantic avalanche. There are days when I avoid phone calls from Penny Axtens, Sony Classical's PR manager. Fortunately she has enough of a sense of humour to take in good part the nickname that I have given her: Hydra. As soon as one request has been turned down, another two spring up in its place.

'Phenomenally talented'

Is he singing too much? Perhaps he did at certain periods. But what can really leave him feeling tired is not the singing itself but all the trappings that go with it. If all goes well, then surges of adrenalin and feelings of happiness can make up for the lack of energy that results from physical effort and mental concentration. But where is the artist who feels unalloyed joy at interviews, press conferences, record signings and photoshoots? Most singers are left feeling more exhausted by half a day of PR work than they are by a performance, which is only logical since there are no intervals, so they have to perform for four hours non-stop. And however annoyed they may be, they still have to remain amiable.

For this reason if for no other, I can fully understand Alan Green when, faced with Jonas's endless PR activities, he asks whether the singer really wants to do all of this and whether he needs to do it at all. Kaufmann should be able to concentrate fully on singing. Green is aware, however, that it is sometimes hard to hold Kaufmann back if he is particularly determined to do something. Green worries about this. Since he started to go to the opera he hasn't known a tenor who can do everything that Kaufmann does: German, Italian and French roles, lyric parts alternating with dramatic ones, song recitals and now popular songs from the era of the early talkies and a speaking role in a film. 'Where else can one find all of this in a single singer? In most cases something is missing.' Green recalls the singer's first lieder recital at Carnegie Hall: 'an eightfold *pianissimo* in this huge space, with people sitting on the edge of their seats – it was unforgettable!' There is, Green concludes, 'no one with Kaufmann's abilities. And yet this in itself represents something of a problem.'

In other words, expectations are so high that every cancellation seems like the end of the world. Fans have booked their tickets and made travel arrangements, in some cases taking time off work – and all in vain. The more famous and admired the artist, the greater the disappointment, which not infrequently turns to suspicion and feelings of hostility, as is clear from various social networks like Facebook and Twitter. But what should a singer do if he or she is ill? Should they still sing and risk permanent damage? Vocal cords are irreparable. There is a long list of singers who were forced to end their careers prematurely because they allowed themselves to be browbeaten into singing when their health was not the best. That is why the first rule of singing is this: sing only when you are really well!

Jonas has consistently taken this rule to heart – even when it took him several months to recover completely. That happened in May and June 2012 and from September to December 2016. On those occasions many people thought that it was the beginning of the end. And in his worst moments he even believed that himself.

'The management regrets...'

The singer as athlete

Singers are athletes and, like athletes, they have to lead lives that are conducive to the health of both body and mind. Unlike sportsmen and women, however, singers do not enjoy the collective sympathy of an entire nation if they have to cancel. A broken leg or a torn muscle fibre – everyone can understand that the athlete cannot compete. But when the voice is not working as well as it ought to, this is the perfect breeding ground for speculation, imagination and doubt: is he singing too much, is he travelling too much, does he have too much stress, too much pressure, has he perhaps had a row with the director? All of this is more readily believed than the banality of an infection. Of course, it is clear from the reaction of fans on social media that there are many who simply wish the singer a speedy recovery and tell him to 'Get well soon!' But at the same time there are always prophecies of doom, insinuations and reproaches that invariably make themselves heard. Perhaps this is in part due to the fact that the clichés and caricatures of oversensitive singers have become lodged in people's minds more obdurately than the tragic instances of singers losing their voices and ending their careers prematurely. My God, these oversensitive creatures who insist on moving to another restaurant table at the least draught and who are forever afflicted by a slight cough, forever sucking throat lozenges! Real sportsmen and women are made of sterner stuff and don't make such a fuss.

It might help to break down prejudices if the process of singing were not reduced to vocal cords, larynxes and resonance chambers. Professional singers sing with their whole body, so it is not enough if just the larynx is working – the whole body has to work. Kaufmann has always stressed this aspect of his profession, not only in interviews but also when teaching young singers. 'If I want to be certain that my voice is working, I need to ensure before the performance that my body is in a position to achieve the desired result, which I do through keep-fit exercises, yoga, and stretching and relaxation exercises. I've developed a particular training programme, and if I follow it rigorously I don't have to waste too much time warming up in the evening as I have already created the physical and mental conditions that I need to be able to sing.'

Two months' rest

An inflammation in the region of the ears, nose and throat means only one thing: the singer has to cancel and take time to recover. In most cases it will be two weeks before he or she is ready to perform again, although in the case of persistent infections and relapses it can take as long as two months. This is what happened to Jonas in May and June 2012. The fact that he had to cancel a second run of performances of *Die Walküre* at the Met, a concert in Puerto Rico and, ultimately, a new production of *Les Troyens* at Covent Garden was already bad enough, but the situation was made far worse by the pressure under which he placed himself.

A terrible situation: you'd been in New York and Puerto Rico with nothing to show for it. Your voice wasn't working, you were running from one doctor to the next, and in London you were urgently needed for one of the most difficult parts in the entire tenor repertory, Énée in Les Troyens.

I was really rattled, I'd never known anything as persistent as this before. And of course I was worried about what I'd do if I didn't get better. It was with a heavy heart that I eventually took the decision to withdraw from the new production of *Les Troyens*. From then on things got noticeably better. There was no longer this pressure of feeling that I was being forced to do it.

A number of contributors to various chatrooms spitefully claimed that you'd not started to learn the role until the very last minute and only then discovered that the part was too difficult for you.

On this occasion I'd actually started to learn it too soon, at least when judged by my own standards. Even before flying to New York I'd already got the whole part under my belt, and although it's not an easy sing, learning it had been so much fun that I was very much looking forward to the new production in London. But it would have been sheer madness to sing it while I was unwell: it's hard enough when you're fully fit. On my return from New York I tried to sing a couple of phrases and it became clear that I could forget the whole thing. It was a very difficult time for me. Sometimes I was so depressed that I talked to Margarete and wondered what we'd do if my voice never worked as it used to do. This was also the time when our daughter was confirmed: I can still recall thinking a lot about how often I'd missed important occasions in the lives of my children as I'd always been tied up professionally elsewhere. Needless to add, my mood didn't get any better while everyone was asking on a daily basis: 'What's going on? What has his doctor said? Is he getting any better?

What made the situation even worse was your appearance at the UEFA Champions League final in the Allianz Arena in Munich on 19 May 2012.

I performed with David Garrett at the opening ceremony, and many people obviously thought that it was a live performance. But it wasn't. We lip-synched to a pre-recorded soundtrack. If they'd insisted on my performing live, I would have had to cancel, of course, just as I'd cancelled all of my other performances and concerts. But at the Champions League final I had to perform for only a few minutes. And it was out of the question that someone else would have gone out there and stood beside David Garrett and tried to move his lips in time to a recording of my voice. So I appeared – and without a fee! I also insisted that the press officers of both UEFA and the German Football Association publish the true facts of the matter on their websites.

It's clear that cancellations by well-known artists bring out the worst in people.

Disappointment can sometimes lead to extreme reactions. Can you remember the scenes after Chelsea won 4:3 in a penalty shoot-out against Bayern Munich?

I don't think I've ever seen so many grown men crying as I did that evening.

And with us, people are really pissed off when we cancel. I can fully understand that, and I'm sorry – but what am I supposed to do? What really annoys me are the insinuations and rumours that are spread by chatrooms and unfortunately also by the press. The claims purporting to give the true reason for my two-month absence were simply outrageous and amounted to a game of Chinese whispers. They ranged from a cyst on my vocal cords to a pharyngeal infection to cancer. This last-mentioned claim presumably related to the lump on my chest that had been removed eight months previously. Although it had been benign, bare facts are of little use when dealing with people who invariably believe what they want to believe. And people generally prefer to believe in something dramatic rather than anything as banal as a simple infection.

Against the background of all these stories and of your own worries, your first concert after this enforced break was almost like a comeback.

It was an open-air concert in the square outside the cathedral in Linz. Jochen Rieder conducted the Linz Bruckner Orchestra and Barbara Rett was the presenter. Yes, this day – 14 July 2012 – really did feel like a comeback. 'I'm back, I feel great, as does my voice.' I can still remember how relieved I was.

Dolce Vita *and a streak of bad luck*

Even harder was what happened to you in 2016, when you had to endure several enforced breaks, all of them in connection with a project that should have brought you a good deal of pleasure: Dolce Vita, *a collection of popular Italian songs ranging from Leoncavallo's* Mattinata *to Lucio Dalla's* Caruso.

Yes, it's really quite strange, considering that Italy had previously brought me so much happiness. It began in January with an infection following the recording sessions in Palermo, with the result that I unfortunately had to cancel the production of *Manon Lescaut* at the Met as well as several concerts. In early July we recorded large sections of the *Dolce Vita* album for German television at the Teatro Carignano in Turin. On the final evening I noticed that my voice wasn't flowing as freely as it should have done – and by the next day I was so hoarse that I had to cancel two concert performances of *Die Walküre* in Baden-Baden. Fortunately my voice recovered relatively quickly, so I was fit again by the time of the next concerts in

Baden-Baden – mixed opera programmes with Anja Harteros, Ekaterina Gubanova and Bryn Terfel.

I then visited Latin America in August 2016 for the first time, giving concerts and recitals in Buenos Aires, São Paulo, Lima and Santiago de Chile. The huge distances covered meant that touring this fascinating continent was tiring, but my voice was working well. So I enjoyed the acoustics of the Teatro Colón in Buenos Aires, which are every bit as phenomenal as many singers have said. Following my final song recital in Santiago de Chile on 18 August, I went on my summer holidays in very good mood. My first appearance after the summer break was at the Teatro San Carlo in Naples on 12 September, an event organized by the publishers of the daily *Il Mattino*, with a guest list that included almost every famous Italian starting with the president, Matteo Renzi. The media circus surrounding it was enormous: a forty-page supplement to *Il Mattino* devoted exclusively to me, umpteen camera crews and so on and so forth. It was an ideal opportunity for us to promote our *Dolce Vita* album. After an open Q&A session for music conservatoire students, which took place in the opera house and took more than two hours, my contribution to the 'VIP Evening' in the Teatro San Carlo was a public interview with Alessandro Barbano, the paper's editor-in-chief, after which I was supposed to sing a couple of songs from my new album accompanied at the piano by Stellario Fagone. Even while I was warming up, I noticed that my voice wasn't very responsive, but I just assumed it was still in holiday mode and that it would be all right on the night. Unfortunately this wasn't the case. I think I've rarely suffered as much as I did during these few songs. To make matters worse, the whole thing was broadcast live on the radio without our approval. In short, the evening was ill-starred from the outset. I was in the worst possible mood, and the next day my voice was completely hoarse. I assumed that it was the start of an infection, but the findings of the medical examination unfortunately proved devastating: a haematoma on one of my vocal cords. A small blood vessel had burst. 'Bleeding of the vocal cords' sounds so dramatic, but there's no blood coming out; in fact it's a tiny injury, comparable to spider veins on your legs, except that for a singer it affects the most sensitive part of your anatomy. You can't sing with this condition. You have to wait till the haematoma has gone completely and the blood vessel has fully healed.

How long does that normally take?
Several weeks. That it would take several months in my own case was something that no one could have predicted. If I'd known this in advance, I could have ensured that this extended break was properly structured. Instead, I went from one doctor's appointment to the next, always hoping that things were getting back to normal.

The only positive thing to come out of this enforced break was the fact that I had time for my family in ways that I'd never had before, and I took full advantage of this. Even so, everything was overshadowed by the concern that my voice might never return to normal.

You returned to the stage in January 2017 for Lohengrin *at the Opéra Bastille in Claus Guth's production from La Scala. Were you nervous?*
Of course. When you haven't sung for a long time, you're naturally worried in case you can't get through the evening. During the rehearsals and the premiere I may have sung with the handbrake on, so to speak, singing more cautiously than usual, less spontaneously, less inclined to give my all. But things got better in time for the following performances, thank God. You know, in *Lohengrin* there many passages where vocal restraint isn't at all possible. You have to show your true colours, especially in the last act.

'Retour triomphal', 'Kaufmann again on top form' – these head-lines after the first night in Paris are an indication of the positive response to your 'comeback', and there was an equally powerful reaction to your song recital and Act One of Die Walküre *at London's Barbican Centre. The performances of* Andrea Chénier *in Munich and Paris likewise left the impression that all is well once again. But in spite of all the relief, there must still be a residual worry in some people's minds: 'Let's hope he takes better care of himself in future and doesn't fall back into his bad old ways.' Is this a justified concern?*

Not in terms of my singing, I think that I've always been very careful there. But in terms of the time off between performances I shall now have to handle my resources with greater awareness and make sure that my batteries are properly recharged. I think that this long break was also an expression of something that all of us basically should know but which we are often reluctant to acknowledge in time: if you don't allow your body the time that it needs to recover, then it may force you to do so by falling ill. To that extent the term 'enforced break' is very much the right one. And one should be grateful to one's body when it applies the emergency brake in this way instead of hitting a brick wall.

Accidents onstage

Someone should really write a book about onstage accidents in order to show how much singers have to put up with. Three examples out of hundreds: Risë Stevens finished a performance of Carmen *with a dislocated shoulder, Hans Beirer sang Siegfried in* Götter-dämmerung *with two cracked ribs, and Jonas Kaufmann continued with a performance of* Don Carlo *in Munich in spite of a deep cut.*
It happened during the auto-da-fé: I'd approached the King with my sword drawn, after which I was arrested by the guards

and led away. The guards were being played by a new set of extras and the two who held me down clearly hadn't seen that they were pressing me against the tip of my dagger. And it wasn't a trick dagger that retracts when used but a historic weapon that pierced my side. During the interval the wound was disinfected and treated, but the dressing made it difficult to get to the end of the performance. Equally tricky was a performance of *Parsifal* in Vienna. I was contracted to sing three performances but had to cancel the first two because of a cold. At the third I initially thought I could do it, but in the middle of the first act I started to have problems with my circulation. I went to sit in the corner by the portal and recovered, but the same thing happened again towards the end of the act. That evening it became clear to me once again how important it is to be able to say no, especially when you are in frail health. In situations like that it's vital that you're fully recovered before re-exposing yourself to the daily pressures of our profession.

What do you do – or what do you not do – to ensure that your body recovers?
I sleep a lot, read a lot, watch television and enjoy simply being able to spend the day as I like. I can do this best on the day of the performance, since it means that there's just an opera or a concert in the evening and I don't have any interviews, rehearsals, fittings or photoshoots. All of this is important, of course, but it takes an incredible amount of time and is far more tiring than you'd think. A photoshoot is exhausting.

I sometimes have the impression that singing helps you to recharge your batteries, rather than draining them.
That's often the case. Singing gives me such immense pleasure that there are times when I simply can't wait till the next performance. It's hard for me to find the right balance. I'm so often pumped up or my adrenalin level is so high that I simply

don't notice how tired I am. For a while the body can cope with this, but the voice is a very fragile instrument: once it has been damaged, this may spell the end of a singer's career. In other words, even when it is functioning at its best and giving you lots of pleasure and ensuring that you're successful, you still have to keep on thinking about how to preserve it for as long as possible. You're constantly caught between these two extremes.

On average, how many performances do you give in a season?
Between sixty and eighty. The most important thing is to choose wisely. But I'm like a kid in a candy store and want to try everything.

And how do you avoid ruining your digestion?
By repeatedly forcing myself to see reason and telling myself that if I accept too many offers, I shouldn't be surprised if at the end of the day I'm completely exhausted. Or, to look at it from a more positive perspective: we singers are in a good position because our bodies immediately tell us if we're taking on too much. Unlike most other people who are in work, we have a fairly reliable early warning system.

Smoke, germs, reflux

Apart from cigarette smoke, what is the worst thing for the voice?
Artificial smoke onstage. It can dry out your mucous membrane, so you suddenly find yourself without any strength left in your voice. But you can protect yourself by drinking lots of water. On performance days I drink up to five litres, lightly salted, which also helps to wash mineral products from your system.

How do you guard against colds?
I always have my first-aid kit with me, including an inhaler and a humidifier. And I dress so as to protect myself against the cold and draughts. But it would be absurd – and also pointless – to go around wearing a face mask. When our children were still very small, it was practically impossible to avoid the risk of infection. When children are ill, they naturally need more attention than they otherwise do – as their father I can't simply say: 'Take your bacterial breeding grounds elsewhere!' Similarly after a performance, when you're shaking hundreds of hands, it's impossible to protect yourself from every germ. If you catch something, that's just hard luck.

What pleasures do you have to forgo for the sake of your voice?
I largely have to abstain from alcohol. I have the odd glass of beer or wine and I also love a good gin and tonic, but I can't enjoy them as uninhibitedly as someone with an office job. With me there's always the unspoken question: how will my voice sound tomorrow? The same thing applies to anything with lots of sugar in it, which I have to avoid late at night because of acid reflux. This is a typical singers' illness: as a result of your breathing technique or, rather, because of the pressure on your diaphragm, your stomach is pushed upwards and the lower oesophageal sphincter that cuts off the stomach is prevented from operating properly. This produces heartburn. Some singers have even undergone medical procedures. I've found an osteopath, a holistic healer who helps me to realign my stomach. It's fairly painful, but it works.

And what about talking? There are lots of singers who don't speak on the day of the performance, or at best they whisper.
I could never do that! Even as I child I could never be quiet. Karin Joussen is an ear, nose and throat specialist who recently said to me: 'Yes, yes, you really can't stop talking.' Once, during

my student days, I was in such bad shape vocally that she told me I mustn't speak for two weeks. After ten days I returned to her practice, which is always overrun with people, and I had to wait for up to two hours in her waiting room. I spent the time working on a role with a friend. When I finally went into her consulting room, she greeted me with the words: 'Was that you who was outside, talking all the time? Can't you remember what I said at our last meeting?'

Verdi and Wagner

Inaugurazione

The hottest day in Milan is 7 December, or at least it is in the Via Manzoni. This is the day on which the city traditionally celebrates its patron saint. Since he is also the patron saint of La Scala, the house's notorious 'Inaugurazione' also takes place on this day: the opening of the new season is one of the major events in the cultural life of Italy. Once a year everyone who is anyone comes to Milan, where they are joined by camera teams, paparazzi and curious onlookers.

For a long time it was one of La Scala's unwritten rules that the season would open with an Italian opera and an Italian cast – though it was sometimes necessary to turn a blind eye to the singers' actual origins. Take Maria Callas, for example. True, she was born in New York to Greek immigrants, but she was married to an Italian, lived in Italy and above all was as much at home in Italian roles as genuine Italian singers.

When Callas fell out with La Scala's general manager, Antonio Ghiringhelli, and Renata Tebaldi was unavailable to take over, an adequate Desdemona had to be found to appear alongside the vocally powerful Otello of Mario Del Monaco on the 1959 first night. The only singer to fit the bill was Leonie Rysanek. She had been the star of the evening when *Otello* had been performed at the Vienna State Opera in April 1957 in spite of the presence in the cast of Del Monaco and of Karajan in the orchestra pit.

It made sense, therefore, to invite her to open the season in Milan. She was duly invited, albeit with considerable misgivings: Rysanek was Austrian, and the conflict in the South Tirol was then particularly intense. Although she won over the audience at La Scala, the press remained reserved, arguing that however well she may have sung, she was more at home in German roles.

Conversely, there was still a simmering resentment in Vienna: because of the contractual agreement between the Vienna State Opera and La Scala guaranteeing greater co-operation between the two companies, the repertory system in Vienna was becoming increasingly Italianized. Verdi and Puccini were now performed in Italian, not German, and Karajan set great store by ensuring that Vienna's casts were as idiomatic as possible, which meant flying in stars from La Scala on a regular basis. The result was that a number of local favourites were underemployed. The globalization of opera had begun, not least through international recordings, and Karajan wanted to show that his house could easily stand comparison with La Scala and with the Met.

The German–Italian border

The degree of sensitivity felt by the Viennese in the face of this 'invasion' of Italian singers may be illustrated by an episode which occurred during the first night of a new production of *Die Fledermaus* on 31 December 1960. The conductor was Karajan. Among the guests at Orlofsky's party in Act Two was Giuseppe di Stefano. As Falke, it was left to Walter Berry to present the visiting singers. He introduced di Stefano with the words: 'He's singing a Neapolitan folksong for us – in Italian!' His comment triggered demonstrative laughter, except on the podium, where Karajan remained stony-faced. The conductor later took Berry to one side and told him to desist from any such allusions in future.

The border between Wagner and Strauss on the one hand and

Verdi and Puccini on the other may have been carefully guarded elsewhere, but at the Met it was already witnessing a number of incursions. The house's general manager, Rudolf Bing, who was Viennese by birth, had no problem using Josef Metternich – the 'most Italian of German baritones' – in Verdi roles: following Metternich's successful debut as Don Carlo in *La forza del destino* alongside Richard Tucker and Zinka Milanov, the German baritone was regarded as an appropriate choice for Italian roles at the Met. Nor did Bing hesitate to cast Leonie Rysanek as Lady Macbeth after his falling-out with Callas. Since then well over fifty years have passed, and in most international houses it is no longer a problem if German and Austrian singers appear in Verdi and Puccini.

Only at La Scala are the battle lines still clearly drawn, but Kaufmann, the Italophile from 'Monaco di Baviera', is well placed to transcend them. In 1999 who would have thought that the Jaquino in that year's *Fidelio* would return to La Scala eight years later as Alfredo in *La traviata* and that he would open the 2009–10 season as Don José in *Carmen* and launch the 2012–13 season as Lohengrin? Even a seasonal opening with Kaufmann in Verdi or Puccini now seems to be within reach – certainly since his Puccini concert on 14 June 2015, an occasion acclaimed by the Milanese audience at such length and with such enthusiasm that it was even reported on Italian television.

However much this may confirm Kaufmann's status as an international artist, he himself seems to regard it as a far more important challenge to reconcile the alleged differences between the German vocal tradition on the one hand and the Italian art of singing on the other: Verdi and Puccini, he believes, need to be combined with the profundity of 'poets and thinkers', Wagner and Strauss with Italianate melody and Mediterranean sensuality.

Against this background it makes perfect sense that Kaufmann made his international breakthrough with *La traviata* at the Met before his potential for Wagner had been recognized in Germany. On the one hand, this is an instance of the age-old tale of artists who are properly valued in their own country only after they have become famous abroad, but at the same time it is the best thing that could have happened to him as a singer, for only in this way could he establish the art of bel canto as a basis for singing Wagner. In this context Kaufmann has repeatedly stressed how important it is to switch frequently between German and Italian roles. He deliberately chose to sing Alfredo before his debut as Lohengrin at the 2009 Munich Opera Festival and to perform Cavaradossi immediately before his Bayreuth debut, also as Lohengrin, in 2010.

Bel canto for Wagner

You've always resisted being pigeonholed as a 'Wagner singer' or a 'Verdi tenor', arguing not only that you'd find it boring to travel the world always singing the same roles but, more importantly, that the different languages and styles, far from getting in each other's way, actually benefit one another. What does this mean in practical terms for the switch between Verdi and Wagner, both of whom celebrated their bicentenaries in 2013?

In terms of vocal technique, I'd very much recommend switching between Wagner and Verdi: after singing Wagner you have an extra helping of power to deal with the drama of Verdi, and after singing Verdi, you'll find it easier to sing Wagner in the way in which Wagner himself wanted: with Italian legato. We know that Wagner didn't like the sort of declamatory approach to the vocal line that was cultivated in Bayreuth after his death and that George Bernard Shaw allegedly once dismissed as the 'Bayreuth bark'. True, Wagner emphasized the need for clear articulation and eloquence, but not at the cost of an inferior vocal quality.

Why do singers so often bellow in Wagner? Is the orchestration too thick? Do conductors take too little account of the singers?
If they are conductors who understand less about voices and opera than they do about symphonic music, then this can easily happen. But they need only look at the scores, where there are lots of *piano* and *pianissimo* markings. Wagner demands a soft, restrained and internalized tone just as frequently as he demands singing at full volume. And in an age when the sources are routinely examined in detail, we should also read what Wagner himself has to say in his letters. He writes, for example, that an Isolde shouldn't sound as dramatic as a Norma. This shows how far we have moved away from the sources.

And how close Tullio Serafin was to them when he rehearsed Norma and Isolde with Callas.
I'd give anything to hear a complete *Tristan* with Callas. Unfortunately there are only two recordings of Callas singing the final section of the work. And this is bel canto Wagner at its best. Wagner's music has a lot of Italian melody in it, a lot that's very tender and lyrical, as in *Lohengrin* and *Parsifal*. The only time when I really have to knuckle down as Parsifal is the scene with 'Amfortas! Die Wunde!' And that lasts only five minutes. With the exception of a mere handful of passages, the rest is lyrical and songlike, which is also how it is instrumented. And if you really want to sing it as it's written, you need a very flexible voice. This flexibility is enormously important for Wagner, and I believe that it can be maintained only if you don't specialize in Wagner but keep your voice supple by also singing Italian and French roles. You can then 'decorate' your Wagner roles with Italian melos and French tone colours.

In Italy there still seems to be a feeling of prejudice whenever Germans sing Italian roles. How did the press and public react to your Alfredo and Cavaradossi at La Scala? Was there a sense of suspicion directed at the tedesco, *the German?*

To begin with, I had the feeling that people were a little sceptical, but this soon vanished. I now have the impression that in Milan most music lovers have accepted me as an 'adopted Italian'.

Lohengrin *at Bayreuth and La Scala*

When La Scala announced that it was opening its Verdi–Wagner season with Lohengrin *in 2013, people spoke of a 'Germanization' of the company. La Scala, they argued, should surely feel under an obligation to launch the bicentenary celebrations with a Verdi opera.*

I think that's a shame. Now that the opera business has been internationalized, it really makes no sense any longer to ask if Salzburg and Vienna should focus on Mozart and if La Scala should perform Verdi first and foremost. Bayreuth, naturally, remains a special case since only Wagner has been performed there since the Festival was founded in 1876, so to that extent it's misleading to argue, as Italian patriots do, that if La Scala was opening its season with *Lohengrin*, then *Otello* should be given in Bayreuth. In the first place La Scala also performed Verdi during the Verdi bicentenary; second, Wagner's birthday is five months earlier than Verdi's; and third, *Lohengrin* has always been regarded as Wagner's most 'Italian' opera. Even Verdi said as much. It contains countless phrases that require lots of *italianità* and bel canto. Of course, there are also a number of passages glorifying Germany, including two lines in Act Three that are generally cut and in which Lohengrin prophesies that 'Eastern hordes shall never, even in the furthest days to come, win victory over German lands.' Knowing what we know about the way in which Wagner's music was misused by the Third Reich, we are bound to find these lines of only limited interest.

We'll return to this theme in a moment. Following your Munich debut in the role, people very much welcomed the fact that you had brought out the bel canto aspects of the score more than they were used to hearing. In Bayreuth, conversely, this wasn't to everyone's taste.

I don't think it's a question of taste since I'm just adhering to what Wagner himself wrote. When he says *piano* or *pianissimo*, then that's clearly what he meant. And if the orchestral sounds allow you to sing it in this way, I think it's irresponsible not to take advantage of this in the particular acoustic space that the Bayreuth theatre has to offer. But some listeners found this unusual and so there were people who for years had acted as music consultants in Bayreuth and who told me: 'Hey, always this eternal legato, we need more text!' Here two completely different worlds clashed with one another.

That's remarkable when you consider that in Bayreuth there's a long tradition of performing Lohengrin *with lots of legato. Everyone who takes a professional interest in the work knows the famous Bayreuth recordings with Franz Völker and Sándor Kónya.*

Even when you have these recorded examples in your mind's ear, there are still surprises when you look at the score. I, too, was surprised when I learnt Lohengrin for the Munich Festival. It's clearly stated, for example, that the famous line 'Nie sollst du mich befragen' ('Never shall you question me') should be sung really softly. I'd never heard it sung like that, and it really influenced my view of the role. The chorus spends five minutes announcing him as a superhero, and instead of unleashing suitably heroic tones he speaks to his swan very softly and tenderly. Clearly Wagner wanted to counter the hero's reputation as a strongman: it isn't a warrior that appears here but a protector who immediately shows the tender, human side of his nature. That's why I really liked the fact that Hans Neuenfels staged the intimate moments between Elsa and Lohengrin in an intimate way.

By sending the chorus members, who were playing the parts of rats in an experimental lab, back into their cages…

That was a tremendous help. The passage 'Elsa, ich liebe dich' ('Elsa, I love you') is tremendously difficult when some 150 people are standing around and waiting for their cue. Lohengrin has been there for only three minutes when he asks: 'Do you want me to marry you? If so, you can't ask me where I've come from. Agreed? I love you.' Kiss. That's what it says in the score. Of course, you may suspect that his words 'I love you' are just a part of his mission statement, a trick designed to suggest that his only interest is the bigger picture, namely, the welfare of the German people. I'd find that a terrible shame, as it really trivializes the work and degrades Lohengrin to the level of an agent of the Grail community. But I think it emerges from the way in which Wagner shapes this scene musically that this is not the case. To judge from the way he's written it, Lohengrin's 'Elsa, I love you' is far from being an example of lip-service stemming from political calculation but is an expression of love at first sight. Only: how can this be shown onstage? It was a brilliant idea of Neuenfels's to clear the stage in a matter of only a few seconds and concentrate on the relationship between two human beings. Elsa has never previously set eyes on Lohengrin; this is the first time she has done so. And when she does, it moves him to the very depths of his being, and so he says: 'I love you.'

Neuenfels is fond of animal allegories. When, in the run-up to the first night of Lohengrin, *it emerged that this time it would be rats populating the stage, I was repeatedly asked if you would go along with this.*

You have to give things a chance, you need to be patient and not say in advance: 'What? Nothing but rats? I won't do it!' It was a part of Neuenfels's concept that there are symbols that can be interpreted in very different ways. One interpretative possibility is that people can always be seduced, you can do anything you like with them. During the rehearsals some people asked: 'Who are the rats? Are they the Nazis?' I liked his production a lot: it was very powerful and intense, but it was also very ambiguous.

And what was it like to work with him?

It was great. We'd already been in contact for some time and talked about how the character of Lohengrin could be depicted. For him, too, the human side was very important, he wanted to show a tragic hero who at the end walks all alone through the field of the dead. And I think that the audience clearly felt Lohengrin's isolation, his embitterment and his disappointment.

Unfortunately, those have so far been your only appearances in Bayreuth. The revival in 2011 took place without you.

I regret that very much. I'd never planned it as a single run of performances, but the rehearsal schedule for 2011 was repeatedly changed and in the end it was brought forward to the point where I would have had to cancel the run of *Tosca*s in London in order to be able to get to Bayreuth. And I couldn't bring myself to do that since Angela Gheorghiu, Bryn Terfel, Tony Pappano and I had been looking forward for a long time to this *Tosca* and its documentation on DVD. We tried to talk the matter through, but in the end we received a reply from Bayreuth: 'We've got someone else to sing Lohengrin, thank you very much.'

That sounds a bit like the arrogant attitude on the part of La Scala's general manager, Antonio Ghiringhelli who, following his row with Callas, said: 'Singers come and go, but La Scala remains.'

But we didn't have a row. Only differing views on legato and diction. Perhaps they thought me too brash, I don't know. The first time they approached me, I had the audacity to ask who was singing Elsa, who was conducting and so on. They weren't particularly amused to find me interfering in this way, but I'd told them very clearly that I'd agree to appear only under certain conditions, because at that point I'd yet to sing Lohengrin. Munich might already have been under discussion, but nothing had been signed. It was terra incognita for me, so I couldn't say: 'Fine, I'll do it, no matter who it's with.'

If Bayreuth were to invite you back, which role would you agree to sing?

I'd be attracted to Tannhäuser above all. It would undoubtedly be a wonderful experience to sing this role for the first time in Bayreuth's special acoustics. The whole house is one big sounding board. You sense that every note is in good hands, and since the pit is covered, you don't have to contend with an overpowering mass of sound, an advantage that shouldn't be underestimated in the case of Wagner's dramatic tenor roles. During the *Lohengrin* rehearsals, with the wonderful Andris Nelsons in the pit, I often thought that in acoustic conditions like these it should be possible to achieve even subtler colours. For that reason if for no other, I wouldn't have missed Bayreuth for anything.

There was considerable excitement at La Scala on 6 December 2012, the eve of your third new production of Lohengrin. *Anja Harteros was ill, as was her cover Ann Petersen. And Annette Dasch, your Bayreuth Elsa, took over at the very last minute.*

It was a feat she performed with considerable bravura. She arrived in the evening, spent the morning rehearsing and saved the first night, including the television relay. And she sang and acted as if she had been present from the very outset. Between her appearances onstage she also cared for her new baby, and the next morning she flew straight back to Berlin, where she was singing in *Die Zauberflöte* that evening at the Deutsche Oper.

The director of this production was Claus Guth, who similarly saw the title role as a kind of anti-hero. For your opening phrases you were doubled up on the ground like a foetus, twitching convulsively, almost like Kundry in Act Two of Parsifal: *wrenched from deep sleep in order to carry out a mission.*

Perhaps Guth demonstrated even more powerfully how inwardly torn the characters are and what flaws they carry within. He showed that Elsa, for example, is not just the embodiment of persecuted innocence but also a severely traumatized woman. For me, this is really the only way of introducing Wagner to a present-day audience: as soon as we see their flaws and weaknesses, they become more sympathetic. We know this from the cinema: a hero who never stops winning is boring. Only when he stumbles or transgresses do we feel for him.

How did Guth's interpretation differ from that of Neuenfels?

To put it simply – perhaps too simply – Neuenfels offered many interpretative possibilities, whereas Guth's characters and the historical background were clearly defined. He relocated the action to the time when the opera was written, in other words, the time of the Dresden Uprising of 1848–9. Against this background the militaristic, bellicose aspect of the plot appears in a different light, as a rebellion against the attempts on the part of the Holy Alliance to restore an older and more reactionary type of monarchical rule.

Wagner's ideology, Verdi's humanity

This oppositional attitude undoubtedly makes the tub-thumping of Lohengrin *more tolerable, but what is your response in general to Wagner's ideology? Does it sometimes take away your pleasure in his music?*
No, but there are lines in the librettos that give me pause for thought. Take, for example, Hans Sachs's infamous last lines in *Die Meistersinger*: 'Even if the Holy Roman Empire should dissolve in mist, for us there would yet remain holy German art!'

At moments like that is it possible to ignore the composer's ideology?
Strauss puts it wonderfully well in *Capriccio*: 'You must separate the man from the work.' Even militant Wagnerians sometimes wish he'd stuck to composing and not said or written as much as he did. The bone of contention will always be his anti-Semitic writings and his unduly high opinion of himself. Is a work like *Tristan* devalued in consequence? Many Jewish artists who were driven from Germany and Austria by the Nazis had no problem performing Wagner at the Met – precisely because they were able to separate the man from his work and because in spite of the way in which his music was misused by the Nazis, they clung to their belief that Wagner's works are among the greatest ever written.

In your view what constitutes their greatness?
The fact that they are endlessly fascinating, which is also why they can sustain such differing readings. Take the *Ring*. From the earliest Bayreuth productions to Wieland Wagner, Chéreau, Konwitschny and La Fura dels Baus there has been an incredible range of interpretations. Wagner's music is a microcosm in itself. The more I get to know it, the more fascinating I find

it. And if you submit to its sway, it has an incredible pull that I myself can't resist either as a listener or as a singer. It can be like a drug, as in *Tristan*. But I don't regard it as dangerous. It's dangerous only if you take Wagner seriously as an ideologue.

Do you also feel this pull in Parsifal?
Even more than with the other Wagner operas that I've sung. Of all his works, *Parsifal* is arguably the one with the greatest depth to it. I feel like a diver exploring a coral reef, always wanting to discover more even though he's running out of air. Whenever I'm playing Parsifal onstage, I have to be careful not to get sucked in, especially in the opening act, where for long stretches I've nothing to sing. I really have to concentrate there in order to react to what's going on around me and not get completely carried away by the music.

Have you had similar experiences with Verdi?
Very often. In Otello's monologues, for example. When I sang them for the first time with an orchestra while recording my Verdi album in Parma, I really had to take care not to lose control. Now, you could argue that orchestrally speaking Verdi's *Otello* is far closer to Wagner than *Un ballo in maschera* or *La forza del destino*, for example. It contains harmonies and colours that point well into the twentieth century. To that extent, *Otello* is the link between Verdi and Puccini. But even those of Verdi's operas that revel in melody have this ability to suck you in. While I was singing a run of *Parsifal*s in New York, I was also preparing Manrico in Verdi's *Il trovatore* and was so captivated by the music that I wanted to sing only Verdi. Then came the next performance of *Parsifal* at the Met and I spent five hours immersed in this world. I forgot everything else and thought that I'd found the greatest and the best of all worlds. And so it went on, a rollercoaster of emotions lasting several weeks.

I assume that as a person you feel closer to Verdi than to Wagner...

That's true. With Verdi I don't have to separate the man from the artist, he was a complete artist and a complete human being. The fact that when he was asked to name his most significant work he answered, 'My retirement home for singers' just makes him even more sympathetic in my eyes. As with Mozart, you can always sense the humanity in his works. Of course, his operas are no more apolitical than Wagner's, but their message stems from their composer's humanism, not from any ideology. That's why his characters are never ideological constructs but always creatures of flesh and blood.

Verdi is said to be the composer of the people, Wagner the composer for intellectuals. Do you think there is any truth to this blanket judgement?

Perhaps to the extent that even today many of Verdi's tunes are more popular than Wagner's. Practically everyone knows 'La donna è mobile', even if it's only from a pizza advert on the television. But I'd question whether Wagner is a composer for intellectuals. With most of the people I know, their love of Wagner's music is an emotional one, there's nothing cerebral about it. That's why it's just as capable of reaching the masses as Verdi's music. Think only of the scene with the Ride of the Valkyries in *Apocalypse Now*. Or the Bridal Chorus from *Lohengrin*, which remarkably enough has been played at weddings for generations, even though we know that Elsa's and Lohengrin's wedding night ends in disaster. In a word, Wagner, too, has memorable tunes, but Verdi's are easier to sing along with and in that respect are closer to the people.

After all the rollercoasters of the Verdi and Wagner bicentenaries in 2013, where would you say are the problem areas for a singer and where are the passages that are especially gratifying?

Neither of them is particularly easy but there are, of course, phrases that you always look forward to as a singer. With Wagner it's the quiet passages such as the one about the dove in Lohengrin's Grail Narration or 'Mein lieber Schwan'. With Verdi it's above all the recitatives, since they give you ample opportunity to interpret them, whereas you can never let go in the arias. Here your singing always has to be controlled, otherwise it destroys the legato line. The particular difficulty with Verdi is the *passaggio*, the transition between chest voice and head voice. Here you have to know exactly what you want to do from a technical point of view. With Wagner the particular challenge consists in the need to develop substantially more power and stamina for his roles. For that you need good training, lots of experience and – patience. More than any other composer Wagner demands the organic development of body and voice. For that reason alone you can't have a twenty-three-year-old Siegfried. Or, rather, you shouldn't have one. Even if the singer's voice is big and powerful, that doesn't mean that a young person can stay the course with roles like Tannhäuser and Tristan.

The long road to Otello

You've covered a lot of ground with both Wagner and Verdi. In Wagner's case you've graduated from the Third Squire in Parsifal *and Walther von der Vogelweide in* Tannhäuser *to Siegmund, while in Verdi you've progressed from Gastone in* La traviata *and Fenton in* Falstaff *to Alvaro in* La forza del destino. *And finally to Otello.*

After I recorded Otello's monologues for my Verdi album I was very tempted to sing the entire part – it's simply one of the most exciting roles in the whole of the operatic repertory, and which tenor doesn't dream of singing it one day? But it's also one of the most dangerous roles. That's why I told myself that it was was better to wait until I had enough experience. I was very lucky in having Tony Pappano for my debut. Despite the physical and emotional demands of the role, working with him was such a great pleasure and inspiration. Unfortunately the day of the premiere was extremely hot (apparently the hottest day in London for 176 years) and the temperature backstage was almost unbearable. But the performance went well. Thankfully, temperatures were back to normal for the cinema broadcast, one week later, and I'm glad that this performance has been documented for TV and DVD. Until Otello, Don Carlo had been my most dramatic Verdi role, but it's simply not possible to use this as a base camp from which to tackle Otello. You first need to have sung Radames, Manrico and Alvaro.

Your first Radames was in 2015, initially in the form of a series of concert performances in Rome which were also recorded and released on CD, then a stage production in Munich. You sang Manrico and Alvaro for the first time on the occasion of the Verdi bicentenary in 2013, both of them in new productions at the Bavarian State Opera. What was your experience of these 'heroic' Verdi roles?

As you know, I'm not really interested in one-dimensional figures who fall under the heading of 'the romantic lover', and so I was initially not very enthusiastic about the role of Radames. It was only when I started to work with Tony Pappano, also the conductor of our Rome *Aida*, that I finally began to hear how great this opera is. Manrico and Alvaro had always been more interesting characters for me. Manrico isn't just a lover and a warrior but is also the victim of a difficult mother–son relationship. This was well brought out in Olivier Py's production; indeed, some spectators thought it was emphasized a little too much. For his part, Alvaro is a complete outsider, a mestizo who on racial grounds is rejected by his lover's family. Martin

Kušej highlighted this conflict in an extremely rigorous and theatrically effective way. I also thought that he'd found a valid solution to the main problem in any production of *Forza*, which is the depiction of the war scenes: using images of 9/11 and Abu Ghraib, Kušej and his designer Martin Zehetgruber created a reference to our own day and showed to impressive effect that Verdi's *Forza* is far more than just an opera for singers with beautiful tunes and a silly story.

What are the vocal challenges of these two roles?
With *Il trovatore* it is, of course, the famous cabaletta 'Di quella pira' that everyone's waiting for and that raises the question: 'Will he sing it at its original pitch and rise to a top C at the end?' This cabaletta is one of the best-known circus tricks in the business and everyone who tackles it inevitably opens himself up to criticism. Whether you sing it as Verdi wrote it, without the top C, or whether you transpose it down a semitone in order to be able to manage the final note without too much stress, in both cases listeners react in the same way: 'Aha, he doesn't have a top C.' And so you're judged by a note that Verdi didn't even write, a note, moreover, which because of the rise in orchestral pitch is now substantially more difficult than it was in Verdi's day. In the studio I sang the cabaletta at its original pitch together with the final C, but in a live performance I was unwilling to subject myself to this stress, not least because in Munich it had been decided to do both verses of the cabaletta. So I elected to sing the transposed version, like most great tenors before me, which again raised the tiresome question of the top C. What is one supposed to do when people are fixated on these things? Personally, I find the previous aria, 'Ah sì, ben mio', much more important: this is the moment when Manrico outs himself to Leonora as a sensitive individual who is condemned to play the part of the hero. Apart from that, I regard this as one of the most beautiful arias that Verdi ever wrote for the tenor voice.

Many tenors have given Alvaro a wide berth. What is it that makes this role so tricky from a vocal point of view?

The *passaggio* passages! Also, lyric and heroic elements lie very close together, especially in the duets. If you could find an imaginary ideal singer for this part, it would be a combination of Carlo Bergonzi and Franco Corelli. Of the Verdi roles that I've sung so far, Alvaro is the most demanding but also the one that I find most fulfilling: I could sing it every week. In Munich I had the good fortune to sing with Anja Harteros and Ludovic Tézier, and there were times when we felt a true sense of fulfilment appearing onstage together, so it was all the more regrettable that I wasn't really at my best for the television recording – certainly not as good as I'd felt during the first run of performances.

Why is it that tenors don't find the role of Don Carlo as gratifying?

I guess the main reason is that he doesn't have a big aria. From this point of view, the others have a clean sweep: Elisabetta and Eboli, Philip and Rodrigo. The other factor is that for generations the opera has been performed in its traditional four-act version, so that decisive scenes and important facets of the role have been lost. The fullest version on which I've worked so far was at the 2013 Salzburg Festival, where you certainly couldn't say that the character was sold short. Here Verdi demands the whole gamut of vocal skills, from the most delicate *piano* to the most extreme intensity. A particular challenge is the 'Lacrimosa' following Rodrigo's death. It's a scene that's normally cut and one which in terms of its drama represents a preliminary step on the road to Otello. But the rest of the role, too, is very challenging in respect of both singing and acting; there are so many facets that have to be convincingly depicted: his sufferings, his unrequited love for Elisabetta, his conflict with his father, his insecurity and his introversion. Carlo is a victim in the struggle between human values and the tyranny of the Church and State. That's what makes it one of the most attractive roles in my repertory. And I love the great duets!

Conversation with Jürgen Kesting: 'Ideal for damaged characters'

Reviewing Kaufmann's 2008 album *Romantic Arias*, the British voice expert John Steane noted that 'The more delicate critical constitutions among us will recoil at the very idea of there being anything so distasteful as a World's Top Tenor, but were such a position available and the title to be competed for, there would probably be no stronger candidate at the present time than Jonas Kaufmann.' Steane wrote this long before Kaufmann was crowned 'the new king of the tenors'. In the four-volume edition of his magnum opus, *The Great Singers* (2008), Jürgen Kesting prefaces his portrait of Kaufmann with Steane's remark. Within months, however, he had published a highly critical review of Kaufmann's debut recital, *Romantic Arias*.

The first part of the following conversation took place in 2010 for the first – German – edition of the present book, while the second part dates from the autumn of 2014 and was published for the first time in the second edition.

Herr Kesting, the 'World's Top Tenor' – did the otherwise rigorously objective John Steane go too far on this occasion?
In terms of his artistic qualities and market value Kaufmann is undoubtedly one of the finest tenors we have today: a highly musical singer, a captivating performer, a significant artist. And he certainly has the potential to become the 'new king of the tenors'. I just think that Steane's comment should be seen first and foremost as an expression of his high regard. I assume that

Steane is as little enamoured as I am of these hollow superlatives and of these artistic rankings.

What needs to happen in the best of all possible operatic worlds for Kaufmann to achieve his full potential?
In terms of theatrical practice and of his recordings, he should ideally deal only with professionals who know exactly what a voice can do today and what it may be able to achieve in five or ten years from now. He should worry less about PR and marketing and concentrate entirely on the roles in which he is in his element, roles like Don José in *Carmen*. Do you know the London production that's available on DVD? In general not a very exciting staging, but the final scene is breathtaking. Kaufmann acts like someone who has just spent three nights sleeping under a bridge, someone inside whom an incredible anger has built up. In fifty years of opera-going, I've only ever seen Jon Vickers play this final scene in as gripping a manner as this.

Do you see him as Vickers's successor?
Not so much from a vocal point of view, but certainly as a performer. In my view Kaufmann is ideal for damaged characters: Max and Florestan, Don José and Tannhäuser, Siegmund and Peter Grimes. Vocally speaking, he has two things in common with Vickers: the broad baritonal foundation and the tendency to switch from a full *forte* to a whispered *piano* at the *passaggio*, the transition between the middle register and the head voice. Sometimes, as with the top C in Faust's Cavatine, this may sound like falsetto. In his recordings of lyric roles in particular I miss the ability to bridge the gap between *forte* and *pianissimo*, the *mezza voce* or, in the French repertory, the *voix mixte*. Sometimes it sounds as if he is keen to demonstrate that even with his baritonal timbre and dramatic temperament he is still able to sing lyrically and tenderly. But I often wonder if this isn't an attempt to hide a technical problem. In the case of the Italian Singer's

aria in *Der Rosenkavalier* – I was present at the performance at the Festspielhaus in Baden-Baden – it was clear that he had great difficulty producing a light and lean tone at the *passaggio*.

This was a criticism that you formulated after his first recital album, Romantic Arias.

This falsetto-like *piano* has always made me temper my enthusiasm for the great artist that he is. I'd heard him ten years earlier in a recording of Marschner's *Der Vampyr*: an unusually beautiful lyric tenor voice, the epitome of the German lyric tenor, I thought. Then came the DVD recordings on which his voice was already sounding much heavier and darker – and where you can sense the great performer. Remarkably, however, the media had little to say about him. When Decca signed him up as an exclusive artist following his Met debut, I thought he'd finally achieved his breakthrough and was all the more keen to hear his first recital. Unfortunately, it fell short of what it could have been if the conditions had been better: the portrait of an exceptional singer. This applies in part to the programme: Kaufmann was clearly being presented as a singer with a radiant tenor voice in popular arias such as Lyonel's 'Ach, so fromm' and Rodolfo's 'Che gelida manina'. A less popular programme would have been better and more sensible, allowing him to show off his exceptional abilities. In other words, more 'character' and less of a concert made up of audience requests. And I'm certain that with the right PR a recital like that would have sold even better than this collection of tenor hits. Secondly, the whole thing should have been more carefully produced. With 'visiting cards' like this, you need a producer who can coax from a singer all that is special and incomparable about them, just as Walter Legge once did. This leads me on to my third objection: why did it have to be a studio recording rather than a live performance? I'm convinced that Kaufmann would have sung very differently if it had been live and given a more vital and a more spontaneous performance. One is left with the impression of a singer singing under time pressure and under the pressure to succeed – and one whose potential is substantially greater than anything heard in this recording.

And what about his second operatic recital, which was released in the German-speaking world as Sehnsucht?
Much better. In most respects it is a success. I still have minor reservations about the way he switches to a *piano subito*. But I know of no one else today who sings Florestan, Fierrabras, Lohengrin, Siegmund and Parsifal in the way that Kaufmann does. Or take his Werther: who is there today who could have performed the role with the subtlety and the nuances that Kaufmann brought to it in Benoît Jacquot's Paris production under the baton of Michel Plasson?

There's still a striking gap in his French repertory: Hoffmann.
From the point of view of his acting, this would be an ideal role for him, and there's little doubt that – vocally speaking – he'd be able to manage the heroic sections. But passages such as 'O Dieu! De quelle ivresse' would be problematic since these require a *voix mixte*. I'd advise him to study the role with Nicolai Gedda – or to listen to the recordings of Gedda or Raoul Jobin.

Is it still possible today to play in the top league in opera and yet retain your integrity as an artist?
We all know what can happen to singers who are dependent first and foremost on the laws of the international market, but we are also familiar with the example of Plácido Domingo, a singer who has been one of the megastars for decades and who has none the less remained a significant artist. No, I really do think that popularity and artistic integrity can be reconciled, even today. Perhaps it's a Utopian vision, but we shouldn't abandon all of our Utopias.

*Herr Kesting, almost five years have passed since our last conver-
sation. I assume that you've continued to follow Jonas Kaufmann's
career and listened to his recordings.*

He has continued to develop his potential and his singing has
become even more cultivated and refined – you can hear this
in his Wagner and Verdi albums, both of which are impressive. In Siegfried's Forest Murmurs in Act Two he is Wagner's
ideal, merging declamation and vocal line. The words lie on
the sound, the recitative-like passages sound as beautiful and
as fluent as if they were melodies, and at the same time every
word is intelligible. It's not the sort of *Sprechgesang* that we've
learnt to fear with many Wagner singers but a sort of *parlando
cantante*, completely effortless and at the same time very elo-
quent. His Verdi album, too, has many great and even magical
moments. Among them are two phrases in 'Celeste Aida': the
pianissimo reprise, which he sings with a single breath, and the
top B flat at the end. Kaufmann sings it exactly as Verdi notated
it, namely, '*morendo*'. And he brings to it a sound quality that
is simply bewitching. Alvaro's extremely demanding aria and
Otello's scenes likewise reveal him as an intelligent singer who
has clearly listened to other great interpreters of these roles and
learnt from them.

And what about your live impression of his Verdi roles?
I've unfortunately not seen him live in *Il trovatore* or *La forza
del destino*, but I did see Peter Stein's new production of *Don
Carlo* at the 2013 Salzburg Festival. It doesn't often happen with
this opera that Don Carlo is the central character. But that's
how it was in Salzburg. Kaufmann had an incredible presence
onstage, and the way in which he brought out the character's
neuroses and inner conflict as well as his energy and sense of
rebellion was absolutely magnificent. Some of his phrases have
remained lodged in my memory – it's like hearing the echoes
of hammer blows on an anvil. Kaufmann can sing with an

expressive density and an intensity that are really quite extra-ordinary. And it's more than what you normally understand by 'expressivity': it's a way of thinking and feeling in terms of the music's sonorities.

This 'thinking and feeling in sound' is a prerequisite for anyone singing Schubert lieder.
Well... That's why I was disappointed by his recording of *Winterreise*. When judged by his operatic recordings, all of which show him to be a tremendously accomplished singer capable of the most subtle nuances, I find his interpretation of Schubert's song cycle eclectic. For me it creates the impression of a collection of quotations, an interpretation at second hand. The fact that he later sang the cycle in many large halls that are unsuited to such intimate pieces is presumably down to today's music industry. Lieder recitals for an audience of two hundred are no longer viable for promoters. This is a development that can no longer be reversed.

And how do you regard his album of tenor hits associated with the name of Richard Tauber and with the early talkie era?
In her review in the *Frankfurter Allgemeine*, Eleonore Büning said that she could happily give away thousands of copies as presents to friends and acquaintances, and I can certainly subscribe to that sentiment. In my view Künneke's 'Lied vom Leben des Schrenk' ('Song of Schrenk's Life') has a hint of comic grandiloquence, and it can probably only be sung flat out in the way that Rosvaenge and Kaufmann do. With the Lehár hits, the popular numbers from the early days of the talkies and the cabaret songs, Kaufmann continues in the tradition of Tauber, Schmidt, Wittrisch, Schock, Wunderlich and Gedda, bringing his own resources to this repertory. It requires great skill to per-form these perennial hits with the requisite lightness, and this is something that Kaufmann has in abundance. When you listen

to this recording, you can sense how much fun it must have been for all concerned, and that's by no means unimportant with this kind of music. And last but not least, the album reveals Kaufmann's unique standing at present. At all events, I know of no other tenor currently before the public who could perform such a broad repertory at such a consistently high level.

At home in Munich

'Ritorna vincitor!'

The Bavarian State Opera, 9 June 2009. Almost eight and a half years have passed since Kaufmann's debut in *Così fan tutte*. Since then he has appeared in only three performances of *Die Zauberflöte* in December 2005, followed by another long silence. But with the change of general manager from Peter Jonas to Nikolaus Bachler, Kaufmann's fortunes have changed, too, since Bachler was keen to bring the tenor back to the leading opera house in his native Munich. On offer was an important role debut – Wagner's Lohengrin – in a new production that would open the 2009 Munich Opera Festival. Three weeks earlier Bachler had programmed three performances of *La traviata* as a way for the singer to warm up. Opposite Kaufmann he cast Angela Gheorghiu, with whom the tenor had appeared to such great acclaim in New York. In the event the Romanian soprano could sing only the first of the three performances, but the message caught on with the public and press alike: 'Doubly acclaimed,' reported the Berlin *taz*, 'as a prodigal son returning home and as Alfredo.' Had it been *Aida*, the headline could have read: 'Ritorna vincitor!' – the victor returns.

But the acclaim rose to a veritable storm of enthusiasm following the first night of *Lohengrin* on 5 July, the evening on which Anja Harteros and Jonas Kaufmann were hailed as a new 'dream couple'. Whenever the two of them were onstage together, they made it possible to forget the lack of coherence in the production and the erratic reading of the conductor. And Kaufmann was finally back home in Munich, where his passion for opera started thirty-four years earlier at the Nationaltheater. Whether in new productions or revivals, whether as a star guest in *Die Fledermaus* or as a last-minute substitute as Lohengrin on 3 July 2013 between two performances of *Il trovatore*, the people of Munich loved their returning hero and were clearly proud of him. Presenting his new lieder programmes at the Munich Opera Festival and taking an active interest in the Bavarian State Opera's projects for young people were further reflections of his own affection for the city. He feels supremely happy in Munich. A significant part in this has been played by Kirill Petrenko, the company's general music director since the start of the 2014–15 season. Among Kaufmann's happiest memories of the last few years have been the new production of *Die Meistersinger von Nürnberg* in May 2016 and a revival of *Tosca* with Anja Harteros and Bryn Terfel, both productions conducted by Petrenko. 'Petrenko is a perfectionist but not a pedant. He is extremely precise and may continue to work on further details only five minutes before curtain-up. In this sense it's impossible to calm him down and pacify him. But he's then satisfied with all that happens onstage during the evening's performance – even if he is still thinking of further changes. And he's very observant, listening closely and watching and sensing all that is going on. For me, there are few other conductors who can be compared to him. Only Tony Pappano comes to mind here. With Petrenko I have the feeling that he can support his singers without ever forgetting his own ideas.'

The fact that it is only forty minutes by car from Kaufmann's home to the Bavarian State Opera and that he does not need to live out of a suitcase is an inestimable bonus for him, and yet the decisive factor is the working environment at the State

Opera, his good relations with his colleagues and the love of the general public.

Conversation with Nikolaus Bachler:
'A source of great happiness'

Herr Bachler, how do you explain the fact that Jonas Kaufmann was invited to appear at the Bavarian State Opera in his native Munich only after his triumphs in London, Paris, Milan and New York? Is this a variation on the old theme that a prophet is not without honour save in his own country?

No, I don't think so. As our everyday lives in the theatre repeatedly show, this simply has to do with the areas on which an opera house management focuses when planning its repertory and choosing its casts. I can't tell you the specific reasons why Jonas Kaufmann didn't sing here before his major successes abroad. I know only that while preparing for my first season in Munich I repeatedly said: 'Why don't you have him under contract? The man is an absolute phenomenon.'

What in your view is so exceptional about him?

The mixture of intuition and intelligence, of naturalness and complexity. In this he embodies the ideal contemporary singer – 'contemporary' not in the sense of trends and *Zeitgeist* but in terms of the fact that the world is now a more complex place. In the 1950s and 1960s it was enough to have a magnificent voice. You presumably know the video of a performance of *Forza* in Naples with Renata Tebaldi and Franco Corelli. Then the principal concern was their vocal gifts and their ability to stun the audience with them. That wouldn't work in our own more complex world. Jonas Kaufmann is a tremendously multi-layered artist. And in my view it is this complexity that makes him unique. At all events, I know of no one who could be compared to him on this point.

Is this one of the reasons why, as a German, he has been accepted in Italian roles at La Scala?
Various things have come together here. First, he could pass as an Italian from a visual point of view and, second, he comes from Monaco di Baviera, Italy's northernmost city. Above all, however, it is his feel for languages and musical idioms. I know of few other German singers who sound so idiomatic in the French and Italian repertory. That's why he is equally successful in these very different operatic cultures and – even more rarely – is accepted and acclaimed in these different worlds.

Since you took over as general manager here, the Bavarian State Opera has become Jonas Kaufmann's mother ship. Would you say, conversely, that Jonas Kaufmann is a safe bet for you?
More than that. He is a source of great happiness and good fortune for me. And not just artistically. He is one of those people on whom I can rely one hundred per cent. If you work together very closely and evolve together, it's like a relationship. And one of the basic requirements of a good relationship is that you listen to one another and compare notes. I'm not a fan of the attitude of many general managers who refer to '*My* artists'. I can't understand this degree of possessiveness. A great artist like Jonas Kaufmann belongs to the whole world. All the more wonderful, then, if he has a home. And if this home continues to be the Bavarian State Opera, I shall be very happy.

Conversation with Anja Harteros and Jonas Kaufmann: 'Then you can take risks'

For many opera-goers, Anja Harteros and Jonas Kaufmann are the ideal Elsa and Lohengrin, Elisabetta and Don Carlo, Leonora and Alvaro, Maddalena and Andrea Chénier. The following conversation took place in August 2013 during rehearsals for *Don Carlo* in Salzburg.

Let's start with the million-dollar question. Can you describe in a few sentences the plot of Verdi's La forza del destino?
Anja Harteros: It starts with a dead body.
Jonas Kaufmann: A situation almost like that in *Don Giovanni*.
AH: That's true, in both cases the father dies.
JK: He doesn't want his daughter to start an affair with 'someone like that'.
AH: But unlike *Don Giovanni*, the old Marquis doesn't confront the man who raped his daughter but catches Leonora eloping with a half-caste.
JK: This man is called Alvaro. And if the old man dies, on this occasion it's not murder but an accident. At least that's what it says in the text. Alvaro throws down his pistol and when it hits the ground, it discharges a bullet that kills the Marquis.
AH: But Leonora's brother Carlo believes that the two of them have killed the old man.
JK: That's why they can't stop fleeing. As fate will have it, Carlos and Alvaro become the closest of friends in the tumult of war, without recognizing one another, of course. As you can imagine, it all ends very badly.

Are Il trovatore *and* Forza *kindred works? Both are set in Spain, in both cases the protagonist is called Leonora, and in both cases we are dealing with a tragic family history from which there is no escape.*

JK: That's why I think it's good that we are performing both operas here in Munich within a short space of time. There's a revival of *Il trovatore* in November and immediately afterwards we start rehearsing *Forza*.

Does La forza del destino *represent a step backwards in Verdi's development?*

AH: Dramaturgically perhaps, but not musically. It contains such wonderful treasures both in its arias and in its ensembles.

JK: Since the start of the Verdi bicentenary I've returned again and again to Alvaro's great aria about fate. I've sung it in concert and recorded it for my Verdi album. It's one of the greatest and most demanding scenes that Verdi ever wrote for the tenor voice and I don't think it represents a backward step at all in his output but is powerfully forward-looking, anticipating *Don Carlo* and *Aida*.

What does 'fate' mean for you? Is everything predestined? Or what makes a person the person that he or she is?

JK: Of course there are forces and powers about which we can do nothing. We're all familiar with the 'hammer blows of fate'. But if people believe in something like fate, they don't believe in themselves, which is why I take far more seriously a saying like 'seizing control of one's own destiny'.

AH: Are you now talking about your career?

JK: Not just that, but if you want to discuss the question with reference to a person's career, I'd say that this is made up of manifold components, one of which is good fortune. If an artist believes in fate and says, 'I can't influence things, everything that happens to me is ordained by God,' then in my view he or she fails to take responsibility for his or her actions. I certainly think that fate exists, but there are at least as many situations when you simply need to take active advantage of them. These are the 'chances' in life that people often talk about.

AH: So says the tenor currently at the very top of his profession. God has given you a great voice, you look fantastic, you're in demand – no, you've achieved all of this by your own hard work, of course!

JK (*laughing loudly*)

AH: Of course, you, too, had to work hard, but most people have to work much harder to achieve even half of what you've achieved – if that! As for fate: many people start by believing in fate after something bad has happened to them, a lengthy illness, the loss of a loved one or something similar. And in situations like that everyone asks themselves why it's happening to them and what they have done to deserve it.

JK: Faith and superstition also play a big part here. There's a saying, 'Not lehrt beten' ('Man turns to God only in his time of trouble'), and this always proves to be the case after the hammer blows of fate that I mentioned earlier. In some places in the world the word 'fate' is so charged with significance that people aren't allowed to use it. In Italy, for example, it's still the case that the title of Verdi's opera is never given in full but is always abbreviated to *La forza del*... as people refuse to say the word *destino*, believing that merely to do so may bring bad luck. But for me fate isn't just something negative. The word can also imply unhoped-for happiness.

AH: I used to think that myself, but I'm now convinced that there are lots of things over which we have no control.

JK: I don't think our viewpoints are all that far apart. People may believe in divine providence, but this shouldn't lead to a sense of fatalism. They should never adopt the motto: 'It's all preordained, there's nothing I can do about it.' In other words, they submit to their fate without thinking, so it's just an excuse for apathy – that's something I can't accept.

AH: Initiative is good. But that, too, is a kind of gift, some people have more of it than others.

This raises the question of talent. Is talent really one hundred per cent a gift of nature?
AH: Yes, absolutely!
JK: I think it's a combination of things. There's no doubt that there are lots of people who are naturally far more gifted than we are – it's just that they've never had any contact with classical music, let alone a chance to achieve anything in our profession. But to come back to your opening question: to become what one is presupposes a combination of natural gifts and the circumstances in which you grew up. When related to our own profession, this means that God may have given you the most beautiful voice in the world, but this won't help you one iota unless you learn to make music with it.
AH: You can achieve a great deal with hard work, but you can't make up for a lack of talent with hard work. Either you're gifted or you aren't.

One example of fate as something positive is that the two of you have found one another as artists.
AH: Well, that certainly makes me feel warm and fuzzy (*laughing*).

Where did you get to know one another?
JK: We made our debut together in *Così fan tutte* in Frankfurt.
AH: And you were terrible! Incredibly arrogant! But you sang all right. No, success has been kind to Jonas. When his career really took off, he lost all of his airs and graces. Because he'd arrived where he belongs.

The next opera on which you worked together was Lohengrin *in Munich. There you became a single heart and soul. At least when singing.*

JK: Yes, I think we both sensed at the same moment that this is how it can be if you inspire one another and keep raising your level. When you've got a singer like Anja Harteros standing next to you and know that there's nothing she can't achieve technically, you can take risks and sing the wonderful *piano* phrases in the *Don Carlo* duets as softly and inwardly as possible. And when another singer takes the same pleasure in such refinements, then this in itself is exceptional, and the resultant feeling communicates itself to the audience.

AH: Pleasure, the ability to give – and also a sense of trust! With Jonas I always have the feeling that he never does just his own thing but is always there for me. That's rare in our profession. So it's all the more dispiriting when, at a rehearsal, you reach a level of tension – in Act Two of *Don Carlo*, for example – where the sparks are starting to fly and the director stops you and says: 'A little more to the left!' This is the very definition of a coitus interruptus.

JK: I think that we share the same instinct for emotional tension, which is why in key scenes like Act Two of *Don Carlo* we are able to create these images that are the result of more than just the director's input. And if someone doesn't like this kind of emotion and actively works against it, then at least you have a partner alongside you who understands you: a trouble shared is a trouble halved. Thank God we are both in the fortunate position of being able to influence our working conditions to good effect. To return to the subject, we're able to take our fate in our own hands and contribute actively to our own happiness. And artistic directors who know their business will understand that this is a key to their own success.

To what extent is sensuality an integral part of musical harmony?
AH: Good singing is erotic, and not just in a love duet. Jonas is a very erotic type of person, and that's wonderful in terms

of your partnership onstage. And if he feels only a little of this, then as far as I'm concerned, that's great!

JK (*imitating the voice of a redneck*): 'We'll talk about that later, darlin'!'

AH: When we were working together on *Don Giovanni* in New York, René Pape said to me: 'You've got such an erotic voice.' I remembered that because it made me feel good. So I'm happy to pass it on.

JK: It used to be called 'singing from the abdomen' – in singing, mind, soul and body are connected in a way that people may perhaps know only from intense erotic experiences. That's why singing requires a certain exhibitionism, because experiences like these are normally enjoyed by couples in the privacy of their own homes rather than in front of an audience of millions.

Franco–German relations

~~

The globalization of opera

Globalization remains a difficult subject, especially in the world of classical music. On the one hand, music has the ability to overcome barriers in ways that no political dialogue can, whereas on the other hand the cultivation of national idioms and styles is an essential part of classical music. In the symphonic repertory this applies not only to works with lots of local colour like Smetana's *Má Vlast* or Strauss's *Alpensinfonie*. But the situation becomes really problematical when music is combined with language. Where is it possible nowadays to hear an authentically Viennese *Die Fledermaus* or a performance of *Der Rosenkavalier* in which all of the subtleties of Hofmannsthal's libretto can be heard? And where can one find idiomatic performances of Meyerbeer's grand operas? In the opera business, the term 'international' is seen far too often from its unattractive side, in the form of stylistic levelling and the loss of specific idioms and national characteristics.

No national school of singing appears to have suffered from the globalization of opera as much as the French school, a point that journalists have lamented since the 1960s. To understand that point of view, one just has to compare the Opéra-Comique recordings of *Carmen* by André Cluytens (EMI 1950) and Albert Wolff (Decca 1951) with Karajan's all-star recording for RCA in 1963. The difference will be clear to listeners whether or not they understand the French language: the orchestra and chorus of the Opéra-Comique are just as much in their element as Édith Piaf is in her songs. Karajan's 1963 recording presents *Carmen* as an international extravaganza with great singers – Leontyne Price, Mirella Freni, Franco Corelli and Robert Merrill – who attempt with greater or lesser success to sound idiomatic. In the decades that followed, it became the general rule to seek out international casts, not least in light of the lack of internationally acclaimed native French singers. The situation has now somewhat improved – or at least that is Jonas Kaufmann's impression.

You learnt Italian as a child, but I assume that French came later, while you were at grammar school.
No, at school I had only English and Italian as well as two languages of less use in opera: Latin and Ancient Greek. Since we always spent our summer holidays in Italy, I had no contact at all with France and the French language. That came only during my studies, when we had to tackle French *mélodies*. But little of this actually stuck. When I sang my first French role – Wilhelm Meister in Ambroise Thomas's *Mignon* in Toulouse in 2001 – my French was so poor that I felt ashamed in the presence of Nicolas Joël, who speaks every language perfectly. So I thought I really had to improve. And I have, simply by dint of practice. You have to trust yourself to speak the language in everyday situations and ignore your mistakes and the gaps in your knowledge.

When you first sang Werther at the Opéra Bastille in 2010, I bumped into Alain Lanceron during the interval. He's now head of Warner Classics. Since I knew that he sets great store by idiomatic French, I couldn't help asking him what he thought about your diction. The answer shot back: 'Perfect!'
I was all the more pleased to receive this compliment in that

it was something of a risk to sing my first Werther at the Paris Opéra – in the lions' den, as it were.

How is it that, as an adult, you were able to learn French in a relatively short space of time, when many singers spend their whole lives struggling to master it? Is it hard work? Ambition? Or a special aptitude for languages?

I think that in my own case it's largely a gift that I have for picking things up by ear. I like imitating people and mimicking accents and can easily find the specific intonation. For my French roles I've got a very good coach. Initially I went too far and tried to sound more French than the French, so I had to dial back. A big help for Werther was listening to the recordings with Georges Thill from the 1930s. It's not just fantastically well sung, the text is articulated with a clarity that you can only dream of.

This requires a very specific kind of tone production that's extremely hard to achieve if the singer hasn't grown up with the French language. If you listen to old recordings with Georges Thill, Ninon Vallin, Marcel Journet, Pierre Bernac and others and compare them with recordings from the age of stereo, you get the impression that the French vocal tradition is a victim of the globalization of opera.

That's a complex topic, and you could write a whole book about it. Let me say only this: as a point of principle, I think it's good that people have come closer together in the world of opera and that it's now possible to exchange ideas with artists from very different cultural backgrounds and that with international productions there is always a new mix of mentalities, temperaments and characteristics. This demands a certain degree of flexibility and tolerance from everyone, and it leads to creative processes that wouldn't come your way if you were to work only with the same people in the same ensemble. But however different the individual participants may be, the piece that you're performing should always be a unified whole – linguistically, stylistically and musically. It's not a question of nationality but of artistic integrity. I don't think you have to be born and bred in Vienna to appear in Viennese operettas or to be a native Frenchman to sing Massenet, Gounod and Debussy. You can learn all of this. But it should sound as idiomatic and as specific as possible – it shouldn't be sung in an international, uniform tone where there's no difference between *Carmen* and *Tosca*. Whether the often-quoted crisis in the French tradition is the result only of the globalization of opera must remain a matter for debate, but I do think that the crisis is now over: there have long been French ensembles for French operas, as in the 2010 *Werther* in Paris. My tenor colleague Andreas Jäggi and I were the only foreigners in the cast. And on the podium was Michel Plasson, a conductor who has this music in his blood. He breathed with us, let us savour the grateful phrases and was as pleased as we were when something went particularly well. We were all immensely lucky.

How is it possible to interpret French roles with the linguistic clarity of a cabaret singer and at the same time produce a legato line? It's a question of breath control. If the breath is well supported and can flow freely, you shouldn't have any problems, especially in the French repertory. It's far harder to sound really natural and not sound like a machine. You can't achieve this with clear diction alone. Quite the opposite, in fact, since it often sounds terribly artificial. It's essential that you internalize every word – not only in your own part but also in your partners'. Only then can you really 'play' with the words and merge tone and word. Only then does it sound fairly natural.

With Michael Rhodes
in Trier, June 2011.
(Michael Rhodes' archive)

In the title role in
Gounod's *Faust* at the
Met, with René Pape
(Méphistophélès),
November 2011.
(Ken Howard – Metropolitan Opera)

With Katarina Dalayman (Kundry) in *Parsifal* at the Met, February 2013.

(Ken Howard – Metropolitan Opera)

(*Right*) At the photoshoot f
Kaufmann's Verdi album, April 20

(Gregor Hohenberg – Sony Classic

As Campus Ambassador in the children's opera
Nepomuk's Night at the Bavarian State Opera, 2013.

(Wilfried Hösl – Bayerische Staatsoper)

(*Right*) Kaufmann's role debut as Dick Johnson
in *La fanciulla del West*, Vienna, October 20▌

(Michael Pöhn – Wiener Staatsop▌

With Anja Harteros in *La forza del destino* in Munich, December 2013.
(Wilfried Hösl – Bayerische Staatsoper)

Thomas Voigt and Jonas Kaufmann in the Deutsche Kinemathek during filming
for the television documentary *Berlin 1930* in January 2014.
(Lena Wunderlich)

With this album Jonas Kaufmann found himself ranked even higher than Lady Gaga in the German pop charts.

As John Malkovich's rival in Michael Sturminger's 2014 film *Casanova Variations*.

Lieder recital in London's Wigmore Hall, January 2015.
(Simon Jay Price – Wigmore Hall)

Rehearsing Covent Garden's new production of *Andrea Chénier* with
Sir Antonio Pappano, January 2015.
(Bill Cooper – Royal Opera House)

Goethe, Gounod, Massenet

Three of the most attractive tenor roles in the French repertory are originally characters from works by German writers: Gounod's Faust, Offenbach's Hoffmann and Massenet's Werther. Do you think that the French and German elements have been successfully welded together? Or do you find yourself sitting between two stools, as it were?

It depends. Offenbach's *Les Contes d'Hoffmann* seems to me to form such a unified whole that it would never occur to me to try to identify those parts which are German and those which are French. Even if the Cologne-born Offenbach was branded an 'enemy alien' when the Franco-Prussian War broke out in 1870, he had far closer links to French cultural life than to its German equivalent. His life was centred on Paris, he wasn't an outsider there but was 'one of us'. I really do think that *Hoffmann* represents an almost ideal synthesis of German profundity and French imagination and that the combination of Goethe and French opera is far more successful in the case of Massenet's *Werther* than in Gounod's *Faust*. In terms of its main characters and style Gounod's *Faust* is fairly remote from Goethe, which may be one of the reasons why for a long time it was performed in Germany under the title of *Margarethe*. Conversely, Massenet has succeeded in recreating the emotional world of Goethe's *Werther* in such a colourful and subtly differentiated way that you couldn't wish for anything better. To that extent – and to come back to your question – I don't have the sense that I've fallen between two stools but feel completely at home here, although I have to admit that initially it wasn't easy for me to translate the German text, with which I was familiar from my schooldays, into the French idiom. The character's inconstancy, his effusiveness, his tendency to brood and his slide into depression – all of this needed different colours, but here the music helped me a lot, of course.

In its day Goethe's novella sparked a whole series of suicides. How do you see Werther? A total loser? A depressive? Or simply a hapless individual destroyed by his lovesick condition?
Generally the latter. It's important to me that the audience should feel sympathy for the character. If he comes across as a pain in the neck and as a loser, then there's something about my performance that isn't right. For I find him sympathetic, and I'd like people to understand him. My God, Charlotte is his first great love and he suffers appallingly since he's not in the least prepared for the anguish of unrequited love. The great challenge of the role is to communicate this to today's audiences. If you place too much emphasis on his suffering, you risk having the audience think: 'Yes, all right, get over it.' That's why I try to ensure that the other facets of the character aren't overlooked: his religious faith (for me a key moment is his prayer 'Père! Père!'), his close links with the world of nature and his social awkwardness.

And to what do you attach particular importance when playing Faust?
In terms of both my voice and my acting I try to do as much justice to the elderly, resigned Faust as to the young Faust or, rather, to the outwardly rejuvenated Faust who appears only as seen through the eyes of the young lover. Mentally speaking, he can't be young since in spite of his transformation he hasn't forgotten his previous life and his pact with the devil. In terms of what he knows and thinks he remains an old man and experiences something that many of us dream about: to be young once again but with the experience of maturity. The fact that Faust's dream becomes a nightmare and that he is both a perpetrator and a victim – to be able to make this credible

onstage demands not only subtle acting but also vocal flexibility. And by that I don't just mean the rising tessitura from the baritonal opening to the high C in Faust's Cavatine but also the many different tone colours. The dark and brooding quality of the resigned philosopher must be present in the voice just as surely as the effusive lyricism of 'Salut! demeure chaste et pure' and the passion of the love duet. From start to finish the part has so many colours and nuances that I'd never want to lose it from my repertory.

If I've understood you correctly, you've not yet crossed Berlioz's Énée off your list . . .
No, it's true that it's a very taxing role, but there are three good reasons to sing it: first, I've already learnt it and would like to sing it; second, I've realized again and again that I develop most when faced by particular challenges; and third, Berlioz's music has been close to my heart for years. This became clear to me yet again while I was working on the new production of *La damnation de Faust* in Paris in December 2015. I hadn't sung the role for years, but it was an absolute joy to spend weeks re-immersing myself in this wonderful music.

Natalie Dessay: 'Not even a little bit nervous!'

You want me to say something mean about him? With the best will in the world I can't come up with anything. I felt only envy – and for good reason. We were singing Massenet's *Manon* together in Chicago. It was his role debut as Des Grieux. And he sang with an authority that suggested he'd had the role off pat for years. On top of everything, his French was perfect. If I'd not known that he was German, I'd have thought – just from hearing him – that he was French: it all sounded so natural. I mean, singing French operas is hard enough even for us French singers. What must it be like for a German? But Jonas won't let up until he has completely assimilated a role in terms of its language and style. That's always his goal, and he learns very quickly, above all by listening.

His versatility, his fantastic voice, his naturalness as an actor and his diction – all of this left me deeply impressed. Above all his composure. There he was, singing his first Des Grieux – and he wasn't even a little bit nervous. He was even calm enough to calm me down. Unfortunately I'm one of those singers who get very nervous before a performance. But if you've got a partner like him, then singing is great fun. I heard his Werther in Paris. He was a little under the weather, he coughed in the wings – but then he sang without the slightest insecurity. And although he has a large voice he can sing such delicate *pianissimos*! He's one of the most gifted singers I've ever met. So I hope he never loses his composure and his delight in singing. And I'm sure that he'll succeed where I myself almost failed: finding the right balance between singing and life, between a career and a family.

Christa Ludwig: 'Ecco un artista!'

My late husband, the actor and director Paul-Émile Deiber, was fond of playing records. He listened to music far more often than I did and used to look at all those video clips on YouTube. This sometimes got on my nerves, but one day I sat down next to him at his computer and listened to what he was listening to. It was after he'd discovered Jonas Kaufmann. Our starter drug was 'Pourquoi me réveiller' from Massenet's *Werther*. We thought it was so fantastic that we then listened to everything he'd ever recorded. The next thing we bought was the DVD of his London *Carmen* – and we were completely carried away by the way in which he interpreted the aria and by the dramatic scenes in the third and fourth acts. A fantastic voice and a great actor!

When we heard that he would be singing Cavaradossi in *Tosca* at the Vienna State Opera, we lost no time in procuring tickets for the first night. And I still remember thinking during his duet with Tosca: 'Ecco un artista!' This was truly great art! Not just bawled out into the audience but sung with incredible variety: *piano*, *mezzo forte*, crescendo, diminuendo, *morendo* – everything you could ask for. Even the top notes in his arias were fashioned with extreme artistry and using a *messa di voce* of a kind rarely heard today since so few singers can manage it.

But – and this is in no way intended to belittle a great achievement – I find that in Puccini you really need to show off your voice, something he could easily do, and approach the role more in the spirit of a Franco Corelli: he should simply let rip from sheer delight in the sound of his own voice. There should be something uninhibitedly animalistic about Cavaradossi, and I missed this with Jonas Kaufmann. Presumably he wanted to avoid this *tenorismo*, this barn-storming kind of singing. That does him credit as an artist, but in this particular case it robbed him of some of his effectiveness as a singer.

The next thing we saw was a live broadcast of *Werther* from Paris. Things got off to a bad start since it was being performed in the vast barn of the Opéra Bastille, rather than the Palais Garnier, which is where it really belongs. To make matters worse, the sets were dreary and the production boring. But as soon as Kaufmann appeared onstage, the whole thing came to life. Even in this problematic setting, his charisma shone undiminished. Ecco un artista!

'In the Palace of the Emotions'

Don José

Im Palast der Gefühle (*In the Palace of the Emotions*) is the title that Claus Helmut Drese gave to the 'experiences and revelations' associated with his years as an opera house manager in Zurich and Vienna. As such, the title admirably sums up the essence of opera. And it also applies to both sides of the footlights: to audiences as well as to performers. Magda Olivero, the *grande dame* of *verismo*, spoke of the stage as a magical place in which artists are transformed, slipping into roles, assuming a different identity and living an alternative existence. For many singers, this is the principal motivation behind their choice of profession, the best compensation for anger and grief and the best medicine against greater and lesser ills. To be completely consumed by a character is also an opportunity to forget who we are for two or three hours.

This switching of identity and merging with the character he is playing is a particular theme in Kaufmann's life that is best illustrated by reference to the character with which he has for a long time left the most powerful impression on colleagues and critics alike: Don José in *Carmen*. In London (2006), Zurich (2008), Milan (2009), New York (2010), Munich (2010), at the Salzburg Easter Festival (2012) and most recently in Orange (2015) Kaufmann has been acclaimed as the ideal embodiment of a man whose jealousy makes a murderer of him.

This aria that Don José sings in Act Two – is it a classic admission of his love or the desperate confession of a man who senses in advance that he has no future with Carmen?

At the risk of sounding pompous, I'd say that this aria is a kind of self-therapy for José: by telling Carmen his story, he realizes what is happening to him. He has spent two months in prison, during which time this ill-defined, difficult and even frightening feeling has grown in him, without his knowing what it is. Until then there had been nothing threatening about love: his love for his mother and for Micaëla, his childhood friend. It had all been amiable and platonic. And then Carmen comes along, and suddenly there is a devil inside him, a devil that refuses to leave him in peace. Once he has been released from prison, he simply has to see her. And she so antagonizes him that his feelings erupt. He has to tell her what's happening to him, which is why it's not a classic declaration of love. The basic thrust of his aria is this: 'Look at what's happening to me and at what you've done to me.' He reveals all. He opens up, confessing to her and to himself just how much he has fallen for her.

Because he is so obsessed by the feeling that he has no alternative?

And because deep down inside he hopes that this way he may be able to move her, so that she'll say: 'Well, it's not every day that you'll find someone who is so honest and so vulnerable, I'll take him after all!' So he is all the more devastated when, in his moment of greatest vulnerability, she says: 'No, you don't love me. If you really loved me, you'd come away with me into the mountains.' This way she makes him all the more dependent on her – not because she wants to make him her sexual slave but because she thinks: 'I've got him over a barrel. Also, he knows how useful he can be. Perhaps he can help us when we're smuggling contraband over the border.' At this moment a trace of rationality tells him: 'For God's sake, I must get out of here. I don't want to abandon the military and become a smuggler

174

and a bandit because of her.' But then they are caught by his commanding officer, Zuniga. As a result of this confrontation José is ultimately forced to make common cause with Carmen and her crowd. But, of course, he doesn't fit in with this world at all.

When he realizes that he's just being used, he cracks. How controlled do you have to be onstage to depict a person whose feelings are out of control?
Yes, that's the hard part about it and at the same time the particular challenge in such roles. You have to identify as far as possible with the character and at the same time take care not to be sucked in by the music and by the emotion that you're depicting. You have to be careful not to give more vocally than is good for you and not to do more physically than your partner likes. In the final scene many a Carmen has discovered to her cost what can happen when the tenor flies off the handle – even if it's only a trick knife that he's wielding.

Controlled ecstasy

An old rule of singing is 'Always sing on the interest, not on the capital.' Can this be sustained in the longer term?
You should at least try to do so, though not at any price. There's often the danger that you'll become too emotionally involved. That's the reason why I've waited so long before singing my first Otello onstage. If you're playing a character who is so pumped up, then you need to see sense and say to yourself: stop, it can't go on like this if you want to maintain your abilities over a period of many years. It's not so bad if you're occasionally overwhelmed, but if this happens at every third performance, you're bound to have problems. It's better if you're always in control of the situation. This doesn't mean that you should hold back

during the performance or just mark your part in rehearsal, but, however much you may be looking forward to a part and however much you may throw yourself into a character, you should never lose control.

Is there such a thing as Karajan's 'controlled ecstasy'?
Yes, I think there is, or at least I've experienced it for myself: you immerse yourself in the emotion so deeply that you're completely filled by it and can feel the audience being carried along by it too, while at the same time you're still able to guide it all along the right lines. It's a balancing act, of course, but if it comes off, it's hugely satisfying.

Do you need to have experienced certain extreme situations in order to be able to depict them credibly? Or is a well-developed imagination enough?
The more you've experienced in real life, the better it is for your performances onstage. Of course, you don't have to suffer from tuberculosis to play Violetta or Mimì. And I don't have to be a killer to turn Don José into a credible figure. But I must be able to imagine what it feels like when unrequited love reduces a person to total despair. It helps if you can evoke similar situations in your own life. Every kind of personal experience can be sublimated onstage if you recall the experience and reproduce the feeling that was associated with it. If you succeed, even the sound of your voice changes – in the sense of a credible portrayal. In this respect the singing voice is no different from the speaking voice. If you know someone well and know how they normally speak and if you then hear them on the telephone speaking a couple of sentences, you'll know immediately how they're feeling.

Opera singing as therapy

Is slipping into a character something that happens just once at the start of a performance – like putting on your costume and make-up – or do you have to keep repeating it every moment you're onstage?

It would be great, albeit psychologically worrying, if you had to do it only once, but, no, you have to maintain this tension permanently. If you fail to do so, the house of cards comes crashing down. And the audience notices this at once: it's no longer Don José but Jonas Kaufmann singing Don José.

Unless Jonas Kaufmann is abnormally tense in his own private life.

It's often been the case that I've been able to unwind onstage and vent the feelings that have been building up in my private life. I'm a very romantic and emotional person, and for me the stage is often a valve where I can release the pressure. For me, this is one of the best aspects of our profession: you can burn off your energy onstage and then be able to radiate a greater sense of calm in your private life.

Opera singing as therapy?

Yes, I certainly think it could be called 'paid psychotherapy'. Onstage I have a chance to live life to the full, its good sides as well as its bad ones, without any negative impact on me and the people around me. For me, singing and acting is the best way to sort myself out. I think there'd be far less violence in the world if people had an opportunity to get rid of their aggression onstage. But once again: I mean releasing pent-up energy, of course, not the actual use of violence – otherwise my colleagues would have nothing to laugh about.

Is this 'therapy' not undermined if the director requires you to do something to which you feel an inner aversion?

I think it's entirely possible to fulfil your contractual obligations within a production concept that you may not find all that great, and in spite of this be able to relate to the character you're playing. As before, it's a balancing act, and it all depends on the extent to which the characterization demanded by the director is compatible with the words and music. I find minimalist productions the hardest. I feel the urge to move onstage, I need physical action and contact with my fellow singers in order to slip into this alter ego and feel it as my own. I also need it to build up the sense of interpersonal tension that we mentioned a moment ago. It's very difficult to act minimalistically in highly emotional situations. But even then we singers have a huge advantage over actors: we're helped by the music. The music is our base unit: it keeps us fed with emotion and energy and allows us to build up the requisite tension. And if the production manages to use this basic tension – which the music provides of its own accord – and to offer a credible portrayal, and if the staging and the music form a single entity – in short, if everything makes sense – then the result is the greatest sense of fulfilment that you can possibly imagine. It's like a drug.

To come back to Don José: what are the role's vocal challenges and why is the part so demanding?

Because it combines lyrical and heroic elements. The lyrical sections demand a very flexible voice production and a *voix mixte*; in other words a mixture of head register and chest register. One example is the end of José's aria. You can't possibly sing this phrase loudly, nor will it work in falsetto. Instead, it needs this mixture of head register and chest register. Elsewhere – especially the end of the third and fourth acts – the role demands a powerful, baritonal voice with heroic top notes.

Ideally the singer should have both of these elements at his disposal: the lyrical and the dramatic.

Many a tenor has come to grief on this tricky phrase at the end of José's aria, but does the audience thank you if you bring it off?
I think so, at least a part of the audience. Many listeners know that a soft note in this exposed register is harder to produce than a loud one. Anyone who has heard other tenors produce a brilliant top note here will perhaps think that I'm having to croon it because I can't sing it loudly. But this isn't an isolated note. I could make this note louder if I wanted to – but I'd never do so, except as a joke at a rehearsal if a conductor were to provoke me by asking: 'Well, my lad, can't you open up on that note?' I'd never do so onstage at this point in the work, not even at a concert of operatic highlights, because, as I say, it's a moment of great intimacy: Don José is a broken man; he admits to himself and to Carmen feelings that have been smouldering inside him for weeks. And this isn't something you can just bawl out at the top of your voice.

'Who's got the biggest?'

But don't many opera fans insist first and foremost on sexy top notes – what the conductor Gustav Kuhn once called 'vocal porn'? And there have always been singers who have taken advantage of this.
Yes, who's got the biggest, the longest ... But what's so great about opera is that it appeals on both of these levels: the sensually animalistic and the psychological. There are some phrases and notes that are simply sexy: just think of Franco Corelli or Josef Metternich. And there are those with whom you're moved to the very depths of your being – singers like Elisabeth Grümmer and Kathleen Ferrier. And, of course, there have

always been singers where both of these aspects come into their own: Callas, Fritz Wunderlich, Christa Ludwig and many, many others. This animalistic aspect of singing has its own charm, and it arguably comes out best when the notes are high and loud, whereas quiet notes tend to be more emotionally affecting.

How important is a top C?
Basically I think that every tenor should have a top C. Whether he has it only on Sundays and public holidays or whether he can peddle it around all the time is less important than the question of whether or not he's afraid of the note. I freely admit that after I changed my technique it took me a long time to sing this note with the same degree of relaxation as the others. Somehow a top C is bound up with the idea: 'Oh no, here it comes, I hope it works!' And it takes a long time before you no longer force your voice and place it under pressure but simply allow it to flow freely and calmly as with every other note. It takes a lot of hard work to deal with this fear and build up confidence. The first step is to get rid of your mental block. This works better onstage, as it's easier to immerse yourself in your role and in the music and you no longer have to think whether it's a B flat, a B or a C. You then sing the note as part of a phrase with all the other notes. It can be a disaster if you have the music in front of you in the concert hall and think: 'Wow, now I really have to go for broke.' If you think that, you usually achieve the opposite. But once I've warmed up my voice, I can generally go well above a C, without even noticing it. And once you've reached the point of trumpeting a top C with total enjoyment, then it's a great feeling, no question about it. But, please, only when it's appropriate.

Is it appropriate in Faust's 'Salut! demeure chaste et pure'?
No, this C on the word 'présence' shouldn't be belted out, that's not a part of the character of this aria, because Faust feels the presence not of a Venus but of a 'sacred, innocent soul'.

And what about Jussi Björling's solution in his two live recordings from the Met in 1950 and 1959? He starts the note quietly before opening up. What if the C – even at full volume – sounds incredibly beautiful and gives no hint of being bellowed across the footlights?

These are the legendary recordings that confirm the rule. I think that as a point of principle this note should be sung with the same *voix mixte* as I use in Don José's Flower Song. I once worked on this phrase with a student and he sang the C *forte*. I said: 'It's really beautiful, this C, but it shouldn't be loud.' We then worked on it, and for the first time in his life he sang a top C *piano* and was overjoyed. Broadly speaking, there are three steps to a top C: you have to be able to sing it loudly, you have to be able to sing it softly, and, ideally, you should be able to produce a *messa di voce* on it, although the diminuendo is far harder than the crescendo: only when you can find your way back to your starting point do you know that you did everything right on the outward stage of your journey.

Verismo

To return to the idea of 'controlled ecstasy': I doubt if the dividing line between ecstasy and control is anywhere else as narrow as it is in the verismo *repertory.*

I'm sure that's true. When I recorded my *verismo* album in Rome, I could feel this every day: this music is so thrilling that you give your all. And you have to! Pretending that you're not taking risks but trying to remain within your comfort zone doesn't work here. When you sing this sort of music, your soul must be filled to overflowing with emotions, and at the same time you have to pay an incredible amount of attention and ensure you're not putting your voice at risk.

This was the first time you'd sung the two most popular numbers from the famous verismo *double-bill: Canio's scene from* Pagliacci *and Turiddu's farewell to his mother from* Cavalleria rusticana. *What did it feel like to sing numbers that launched Caruso on his international career and marked the start of the history of the gramophone record?*

Wonderful! Once 'Ridi, Pagliacco' was in the can, Pappano rushed over to me and danced through the studio with me, saying over and over: 'We did it! We did it!' I still remember listening to this piece as a student and thinking: 'Wow, it must be fabulous to be able to sing it!' And so it was. To feel yourself swept along by this music and to give everything physically and psychologically, it was simply great. Even the musicians in the orchestra, who normally take a while to show any enthusiasm, cheered and shrieked with delight. That said, my personal favourite on this album is a largely unknown number, 'Giulietta! Son io' from Riccardo Zandonai's *Giulietta e Romeo*, the scene in which Romeo laments Juliet's death, refusing to believe that she's dead. It's a desert-island number. I don't think it's possible to pack more emotion into a piece of music.

Verismo uses powerfully melodramatic elements and paints feelings with the broadest of brushstrokes. As such it comes close to kitsch.

As an aesthetic concept, *verismo* means something along the lines of 'truth instead of beauty'. The operas from this period seek to come as close as possible to the beating pulse of real life. Unlike earlier styles that made a tentative move in the same direction, sobs and portamentos are not only permitted in *verismo* works, they are positively desirable. And as long as the whole thing creates an impression of truth, there is no danger of kitsch. Take the sobs in 'Ridi, Pagliaccio': if they allow you to express the character's despair, they're fine. But it's a small step from the dramatic to the ridiculous, and so singers have to be very careful about the resources that they choose to use.

Earlier generations of singers used to risk far more in this regard than we're used to today. It can be very exciting when you hear Mascagni's favourite Santuzza, Lina Bruna Rasa, for example. In his recording of Cavalleria *from 1940, she sings as if there's no tomorrow. But this sort of* espressivo *can easily become involuntarily comical if it's over the top.*

There are a number of examples of this sort of approach. By today's standards it tends to sound kitsch, but I wouldn't like to be without it. As testimony to a very specific time and a particular emotional world, they have an unmistakable element to them that reminds me of the German films of the 1950s which adopted a romanticized view of the countryside. And then there are singers whose recordings are so powerful that they've retained their tremendous appeal in spite of the changing *Zeitgeist*. Take Magda Olivero, arguably the most artistic of all the *verismo* sopranos. And Claudia Muzio! Her recording of Licinio Refice's 'Ombra di nube' moved me so much that I was determined to include it in my *verismo* album.

You first sang Cav & Pag *onstage at the 2015 Salzburg Easter Festival: it was your double debut as Turiddu and Canio in Philipp Stölzl's atmospherically intense production. I imagine that it can't be very satisfying to return to the concert hall and sing 'Ridi, Pagliaccio' and 'Mamma, quel vino' when these arias are wrenched from their proper context.*

To sing two great roles in a good production on a single evening is hugely satisfying and can't really be compared to the special challenge of assuming a different role every five minutes at a concert that's made up of arias. Both approaches have their attractions. Of course, a concert can only benefit if you've already sung these arias in a fully staged performance.

But basically I think that as a singer you should have enough imagination to slip into character in the concert hall even if you've not previously sung the role onstage. Whether it's a staged performance or a concert, you're not just performing popular tunes but creating a situation. Or, rather, that's how it should be. When you sing 'Ridi, Pagliaccio', for example, in the concert hall, it shouldn't sound like one of Leoncavallo's greatest hits. Instead, you should be telling the story of the ageing comedian and his young and unfaithful wife in exactly the same way that you would on the operatic stage. Or take Lauretta's aria 'O mio babbino caro'. This refers to a very specific situation. 'If you won't let me marry Rinuccio,' she tells her father, 'I shall go to the Ponte Vecchio and throw myself in the Arno!' Even if this sounds more dramatic than it's intended to be, it says a lot about the woman. She pulls out all the stops in order to get her father to change his mind. And this has to come out, even in the concert hall.

La bohème *with two tenors*

Of the great Puccini operas, it was Tosca *that was central to your activities over a number of years. You hadn't sung Rodolfo in* La bohème *for quite some time when you received a call from the Salzburg Festival on 4 August 2012, asking you to help them out in an emergency.*

It was a free day between two performances of *Ariadne auf Naxos* and I was visiting Renée and Otto Schenk. At ten to eight I received a call announcing that Piotr Beczala couldn't sing. Was I able to take over? I said yes without thinking, even though I hadn't sung Rodolfo for eighteen months. I jumped into my car and raced to the Festspielhaus. While driving, I tried to warm up, which isn't so easy when you're sitting, and in the dressing room I performed a couple of yoga exercises. I then said hello to my colleagues and to the conductor, and off I went to the music stand. And so it was that Anna Netrebko had two Rodolfos that evening: Piotr walked through the part while I sang from the side of the stage. While doing so, I realized how much I'd missed these tunes, and from then on it was a source of enjoyment rather than stress, not least because of the fabulous cast. The next day was the television relay of *Ariadne*.

Wasn't there a similar situation years ago, during a Don Giovanni *performance in Bad Lauchstädt?*
The Commendatore suddenly found himself unable to speak in Act Two. I was the Don Ottavio, and because I have a good lower register, I stood in the wings during the Commendatore's scene and sang, while my colleague just moved his lips. A couple of people said afterwards that it had been a brilliant idea to play a recording of a good Commendatore at this point in the performance.

La fanciulla *in Vienna*

Your next Puccini role was Dick Johnson in La fanciulla del West *at the Vienna State Opera in 2013. Why does this opera continue to be seen as an outsider?*
Perhaps it's the subject matter – goldminers and the Wild West, which nowadays seems to get in the way of our appreciation, not least because of all the clichés that we know from the cinema. But if you rid yourself of these John Wayne images and try to look at the story from the same perspective as *Il tabarro*, for example, and focus on the incredibly detailed study of a particular milieu, then you can gain access to the piece far more quickly. We're not dealing here with cowboys and native Americans but with the worries, fears and desires of failed lives. Above all, it's about the search for the great love of our lives.

Marco Arturo Marelli's Vienna production brought this out very clearly.

And how do you rate the work musically?
Fanciulla is incredibly rich from a musical point of view. Time and again during the rehearsals in Vienna I was fascinated by all of the colours and facets in the orchestral sound. And then there's Puccini's ability to create a very specific atmosphere by means of sudden harmonic shifts. Take the end of Act One, for example: this is music that I find almost addictive. In this regard, too, there are powerful parallels with *Il tabarro*. Each time you think that the harmonies are about to be resolved, the tension is ratcheted even higher. It's really the orchestra that plays the leading role here. Even so, the title role is extremely demanding. The fact that it was Emmy Destinn – in her day the leading dramatic soprano in the Italian repertory – who sang the title role at the work's first performances says it all.

But your own part isn't exactly unrewarding.
No, that's true. Admittedly, it doesn't have the great tenor hits that you've got in *La bohème* and *Tosca*, but it has substantially more nuances, which makes it a particularly attractive role for me. Puccini gave Dick Johnson a very individual musical pro-file: objectively speaking, he's a small-time crook who's grown up in the wrong environment and who's set out in the wrong direction. If there had been something like the Venezuelan El Sistema project during his childhood, he'd probably have become an excellent musician. But in Puccini's opera we see him through the rose-tinted glasses of his heroine: not as a small-time crook but as a fascinating stranger familiar with the ways of the world. I'm tremendously attracted to the idea of depicting this ambiguity.

Puccini with Pappano

Des Grieux in Manon Lescaut *seems almost one-dimensional in comparison, a man sexually dependent on his lover.*

I'm attracted to the idea of bringing out the various stages in his dependency, from his romantic infatuation in the first act to his naked despair in the last. But the particular challenge of the part lies in its vocal demands. Plácido Domingo has described it as even more difficult than Otello. I can't confirm or deny this as I've yet to sing Otello, but there is no doubt that for the tenor *Manon Lescaut* is far more demanding than *Tosca*. The role runs the whole gamut from the lyrical to the dramatic. 'Guardate, pazzo son' is a test for any dramatic tenor, and the other scenes, too, are not without challenges of their own.

For the new production of Manon Lescaut *in London you worked with Antonio Pappano. Can one say that as far as the Italian repertory is concerned he is the central conductor in your life?*

Absolutely. I'm hugely grateful to him for so many things – not just insights into my roles but also moments of great happiness onstage. Our joint recordings and performances are some of the most wonderful experiences I've known. And there's never any stress with him, everything is completely relaxed even when he has a packed schedule. He has an incredible amount of energy. I don't know where he gets it from. And in the recording studio he manages in only a short space of time to create the same sort of tension as you'd find in a live performance. That's what happened when we recorded the great duet from *Manon Lescaut* for our Puccini album in Rome. From the word go there was the same degree of tension as the one that Kristīne Opolaïs and I had built up during our performances in London, even though ten weeks had passed since then. Even the very first take had a drive that made us think we could leave it at that. And you feel in such safe hands with Tony – the sort of thing that singers can normally only dream about. His father was a vocal coach. He grew up with opera and singers and has known the repertory inside out since childhood. He breathes with the singers and gives them fantastic support. A truly great musician and a wonderful friend.

Antonio Pappano: 'To thine own self be true'

'Ridi, Pagliaccio': 'Laugh, Pagliaccio' – this is the cry of a tormented soul, the essence of *verismo*, of realism in opera. It is not beauty and nobility as such that are central to our interest here but cruelty and coarseness, jealousy and hatred, envy and violence, murder! To be able to express all of this without lapsing into a hyper-naturalistic *Sprechgesang* is the particular challenge that *verismo* places on every singer. Enrico Caruso was the first to understand how to combine two things that appear to be total opposites: a classical vocal technique based on the set principles of bel canto and a modern style, a sensuously beautiful sound and high-tension expressiveness, matched with the eloquence of an actor. Caruso's recording of 'Vesti la giubba' is not only a key document of the *verismo* style, but also the beginning of a new era in recording history; it turned the gramophone record into a mass medium. Since then many famous tenors have recorded this dramatic monologue, and every tenor who tackles it invites comparison with the greatest singers of the past. When I recorded this scene with Jonas Kaufmann – it is at the heart of his new album of *verismo* scenes – I was probably more nervous and excited than he was. I'd grown up with this aria (my father was a tenor), so I knew how incredibly difficult it is to sing. But from the very first take Jonas was on such good form that we could concentrate fully on the music and its interpretation. He sang with so much expression and feeling and with so many colours that it was pure joy to be so closely involved. He is in total command of all the subtleties of the Italian language; when he sings, the studio suddenly becomes a stage. He doesn't just sing the notes, he acts with his voice. And it is precisely this that sets his recording of 'Vesti la giubba' apart from many of the others. When you hear it, you can see the scene before you in your mind's eye: the despair of the ageing comedian who has just discovered that his young and attractive wife is cheating on him, yet he knows the show must go on. After we'd finished the scene, we were as happy as schoolboys, jumping up and down, literally!

I got to know Jonas during the rehearsals for Berlioz's *La damnation de Faust* in 2002 in Brussels. My first impression of him was that here was no ordinary tenor. He doesn't show off his beautiful voice per se but uses it in a musical and extremely subtle way, perfect for the French repertoire. I could scarcely believe that he'd been speaking French for only a short period of time; stylistically and linguistically he seemed to be fully at home with Berlioz's tricky idiom. He is a naturally musical person and an intelligent one as well, but of course he's also a stage animal – yet one with taste and sensitivity. It is rare for one person to have this combination of talents, but what has always fascinated me in particular is his vocal technique: it is 'old-school' in the best sense of the term, and his secret weapon.

Since his Brussels *Damnation*, his voice has developed and is now darker, fuller and rounder. I've conducted for the birth of five of his great character portrayals: Don José, Cavaradossi, Des Grieux in *Manon Lescaut*, Andrea Chénier and Otello. Though these roles are all pillars of the romantic tenor repertoire, Otello is something special indeed. Jonas faced perhaps his greatest challenge not only as a singer, but as an artist. I watched him every day wrestle with the titanic challenges of the role, both technical and dramatic. He knew he had to find something more, something new in himself, and after unrelenting perseverance, he did! Each performance gained in strength and profundity, relishing the wonder of this unique new territory.

Working with him is fun, inspiring, and totally natural, without artifice. He has recognized what a great gift it is to be able to live through music and to live onstage and, what's more, to be paid for doing so! Correspondingly great is his sincere respect for the composer and his work – and also for his audience. I don't know if he has a maxim in life that governs his behaviour, but if he does, then it seems to be the famous line from Shakespeare: 'To thine own self be true.'

The performance after the performance

Meeting fans

The final curtain has fallen, and the singers have removed their make-up and showered, but it is not yet time to call it a day. What follows is known in theatrical parlance as 'the performance after the performance', the time when singers meet their fans and are expected to sign autographs at the stage door. Depending on their passing mood and temperament, singers react very differently to this aspect of their work. Often it is a welcome opportunity to chill out: inwardly they are still churned up, their bodies pumped full of adrenalin, and by talking to members of the audience they can slowly come down from a high and return to a semblance of real life. It would occur to few of them simply to slip away and spend the rest of the evening alone in their hotel room. On other days, conversely, it can be a burden: they are tired and hungry and would prefer to grab a bite to eat and then return to their hotel, but instead they pull themselves together since they don't want to disappoint their fans. Very few singers consistently avoid the whole business of these performances after the performance; in the course of their careers, these singers have devised various strategies which allow them to slip away unrecognized.

Jonas Kaufmann, too, sometimes leaves by the back door if he has a supper date or feels under the weather, but essentially he sees these occasions as a part of his profession: 'The audience has spent a couple of hours listening to me and now I'd like to spend some time listening to them. Members of the audience evidently feel a great need to tell me what they are feeling or simply to shake my hand, otherwise they wouldn't spend goodness knows how long standing in the cold and waiting. I'd find it difficult simply to rush past them and call out that I don't have time.'

Anyone who observes Kaufmann on these occasions will note how quickly he can attune himself to the person standing opposite him, whether it be connoisseurs who engage in detailed conversations about music or men and women who make no secret of how attractive they find him. He would rather people get too close to him than risk them thinking that he is unapproachable or arrogant. The fact that selfies have now largely replaced autographs has reduced the distance between artist and fan to a minimum: heads have to be pressed close together for photographs that can be posted on Facebook. Against this background Jonas Kaufmann avoids getting too close to fans during the winter months: the risk of catching a virus and having to cancel forthcoming performances is simply too great. He prefers to deal with the fact that his fans will be disappointed by his absence rather than face their displeasure at a cancelled performance, displeasure which sometimes finds expression in reproachful comments on his Facebook page.

At signings he is his usual self: he never talks down to people, is never guilty of false modesty in turning down compliments and never adopts the stance that he is 'just a servant of art'. For artists, the hardest thing of all is to be natural, but for Jonas Kaufmann this is an integral part of his personality.

Key experiences

As in every section of the population, there is a broad range of behaviour among fans, from nice to disagreeable. There are sad cases such as that of 'Miss N.' whom Birgit Nilsson describes in her memoirs: for ten years the Swedish soprano was stalked by a well-to-do fan who followed her every step. The story ended when the young woman took her own life and included a clause in her will stating that her ashes were to be scattered on Nilsson's farm. While this may be an extreme case, it indicates how dangerous opera can be as a drug for people who have lost their sense of inner balance; fondness can become attachment, passion can turn into an obsession.

So far Jonas Kaufmann has not had to deal with stalkers. Indeed, his experience of fans has been entirely positive, and whenever the subject comes up, it is clear that the people who wait for him at the stage door after a performance are quite different. What looks at first sight like a fan club is often a heterogeneous group made up of the most disparate types. What links them together is their passion for music and a key experience in their lives that they owe to the artist in question: a performance or a recording that has triggered something in them, a feeling that they have not previously known. And this feeling is so powerful that it refuses to go away. They need to process their experience and may write a letter that begins with the words: 'I've attended many opera performances but never before have I felt compelled to write to an artist. But after I heard you yesterday...'

This kind of reaction appears to confirm an old adage in the theatre world: no matter how good or bad a performance may be, the audience will include at least one person whose life will be changed completely by it. At least one person is present who as a result of the performance feels and thinks differently and who proceeds to take decisions that differ from those taken by other people. These may be insights that lead the individual in question to change his or her listening habits, but they may also be shattering emotional experiences of a kind that Aristotle, describing the impact of Ancient Greek tragedy, termed 'catharsis', a purging of the soul. In everyday life tears are generally seen as a sign of weakness and despair, but in the theatre and concert hall they may still have their original, purifying effect. In her famous tribute to Maria Callas, the German writer Ingeborg Bachmann argued that 'so many senseless tears are shed, but the tears that were shed for Callas were not so senseless at all'.

Against this background, letters like the one that Jonas Kaufmann received after his Bavarian State Opera debut as Lohengrin say more about the reciprocal relationship between the artist and his public than any model from communication studies that seeks to define the relationship between singer and audience.

'I've just come from the opera and am still looking rather tearful. I started to cry at the very first bars of the Grail Narration. [...] Tears mean a lot to me since I normally can't cry at all. I suffer from such severe depression that I can scarcely feel emotions such as joy and sadness any longer. But with your voice you are able to lift me out of my depression for hours on end – a further reason to be grateful to you. [...] During the interval I spoke to two real opera buffs who said they'd never heard a Lohengrin who sang and acted in such a moving and affecting way as you did. This was certainly true in my own case. But that's hardly a surprise since – at the age of nearly seventy-five – I am just as much in love with you as almost all of the female members of the audience, whether they be fifteen or ninety-five. I hope you won't take this amiss!'

Time and again the letters that Kaufmann receives refer to the therapeutic impact that a particular performance can have.

'No therapy, no treatment can compare with the movement of energy that your voice can achieve,' wrote one opera-goer from London after seeing Kaufmann in *Don Carlo*.

And not infrequently one has the impression that educated and experienced amateurs are more alive to the details of an interpretation than professional critics: 'Not just a vocal performance that brought great joy,' wrote a Swiss opera lover about Kaufmann's performance as Don José, 'but also the perfect expression of what is going on here: memory, *à la recherche du temps perdu*. This sense of being lost is very much the fate of Don José, *your* Don José, a feeling clear from your body language at every single moment.'

À la recherche du temps perdu: the idea that Marcel Proust expresses in the title of his magnum opus returns again and again in the letters that Kaufmann receives from his audiences: the search for lost time and for a lost art. But in contradistinction to Proust, the irretrievable is preserved in opera not only in the subjective memory but also in 'objective' documents. The invention of the gramophone record has meant that we can now check whether or not our memory is fallible, and in the age of YouTube much that was once irrecoverable can now be accessed instantly by anyone; practically every performance can be privately recorded and preserved for posterity. If the list of Kaufmann's official studio, TV and radio recordings is impressive, the offer of 'private recordings' on websites comes close to being unmanageable, even for fans and collectors.

The 'Unofficial Website'

Marion Tung, who runs the 'Jonas Kaufmann Unofficial Website' (www.jkaufmann.info), reckons that there are currently over five hundred live recordings of the tenor's opera performances and concerts in circulation among collectors. A former tax official,

Tung has always been a fan of live recordings: they document the real thing with all the strengths and weaknesses, all the risks and imponderables of a live performance. In Tung's case, her seminal experience was a live relay of *La traviata* from the Met that was broadcast all over the world a week after the singer's debut. Since then Kaufmann has been one of her favourites and she attends his performances whenever she can. 'Generally one performance isn't enough for me,' says the sixty-four-year-old, 'there must be at least two. I saw his Paris Werther four times. I've now seen around 260 of his performances, including so many unforgettable experiences that I find it really hard to say which are my personal highlights. Off the top of my head I'd say Massenet's *Manon* in Chicago, *Walküre* and *Parsifal* at the Met, *Trovatore* and *Forza* in Munich and *Fanciulla* in Vienna. Of all the lieder recitals that I've heard, his *Winterreise* in Berlin is right up there at the top. What is clear to me again and again from Kaufmann's performances is the difference between simply being in possession of a beautiful voice and being a consummate artist. For me, Kaufmann is a complete artist, since his singing and acting radiate so much emotion that as a member of the audience you become involved the moment he sets foot on the stage. With the passage of time it's become more difficult for me to remain in contact with him, simply because after a performance far more people are waiting for him than was the case five or six years ago. And everyone wants their "selfie with the star". He's often so besieged by fans that I prefer to remain in the shadows.'

Marion Tung plans her opera trips herself, independently of clubs and tour organizers. As a widow and the mother of two grown-up daughters she is completely free to take her own decisions. But even if she books budget flights and puts up at inexpensive hotels, it remains a costly passion. Nor should anyone underestimate the amount of time that she invests in the 'unofficial website'. It is a clearly structured, well-designed site that features comprehensive documentation that I myself found extremely helpful while preparing this book, not least as a result of its almost complete list of Kaufmann's appearances and an extensive collection of reviews.

A Romanian national, Alina Vlad now works for a business enterprise in London. For her, too, a performance of *La traviata* proved a key moment. In this case it was Kaufmann's role debut as Alfredo at La Scala: 'The moment when I became a Kaufmann fan', she says, 'was "Parigi, o cara". It was sung more tenderly than I'd ever heard it before. And at the very same moment I thought, "Why have I never heard it like this before? This is exactly how it should be sung!" In my view one criterion of true artistry is when long-familiar scenes sound as if you're hearing them for the first time. That's how it was with *Manon* in Chicago, *Lohengrin* in Munich, *Werther* in Paris, *Don Carlo* in London and *La forza del destino* in Munich. The scenes in *Don Carlo* with Kaufmann and Keenlyside are among the most vivid I've ever known in opera. Equally magnificent were the scenes with Kaufmann and Ludovic Tézier in *Forza*: in terms of their acting it was tremendously intense and, vocally, the most powerful performance that I've heard since Franco Corelli and Ettore Bastianini. I was less keen on the Munich *Trovatore* but I'll never forget Jonas, especially in Manrico's aria "Ah sì, ben mio". And his soft singing is as spellbinding and unique today as it was when I first heard it in "Parigi, o cara", all those years ago. I'm not really a fan of singing for its own sake; I'm interested first and foremost in music, in opera as a holistic experience, which includes the singers. But when I sense that certain qualities in the music are more powerfully expressed by certain artists than by others, I naturally pay attention to who is singing. And what always fascinates me about Kaufmann is that he doesn't just parade his voice but allows us to hear the inner meaning of the music. He could find success far more easily if he threw a few high notes into the audience, but he refuses to be misled into doing this, preferring to make people listen to him by not availing himself of old listening habits and expectations. It is this that constitutes his particular quality as a lieder recitalist: he's not an opera singer who also sings lieder but an artist who from the start of his career has taken a keen interest in the classical lieder repertory, so it's no wonder that it was through him that I first found access to the world of lieder. In recent years I've heard almost all of the great lieder recitalists sing *Winterreise* in London, but no interpretation of the cycle has moved me as much as Jonas's. I also think that his vocal and artistic development emerges most clearly from his lieder singing. When I think of how he sang Liszt's Petrarch Sonnets a few years ago and how he sings them now – it's a completely different world. At the end of his last lieder recital at the Wigmore Hall, I heard a female singer say that it had been the best singing lesson you could have today.'

Lieder, the ne plus ultra of singing

The magic of the moment

Operatic roles demand the strength and stamina of a top athlete, lieder the sensitivity and fine motor skills of a clockmaker. This distinction has become engrained in people's thinking – with singers as much as audiences. And time and again the truth of the remark seems to be demonstrated in the everyday world of the opera house and concert hall: which Cavaradossi does not struggle to deal with the subtleties of Schumann's *Dichterliebe* and where is the Carmen who can confront the complexities of Hugo Wolf's lieder?

But this is only half the story, for time and time again there have been singers capable of singing operatic roles and lieder with equal authority: Lotte Lehmann and Hans Hotter, Elisabeth Schwarzkopf and Dietrich Fischer-Dieskau, Irmgard Seefried and Fritz Wunderlich, Christa Ludwig and Walter Berry, and Brigitte Fassbaender and Hermann Prey – to cite only the most famous examples. Even today, when singers tend increasingly to specialize in particular areas of the repertory, we continue to find examples of this ability to do justice to both of these genres: Renée Fleming, Diana Damrau, Bo Skovhus, Simon Keenlyside, Christian Gerhaher and a number of others.

But the fact remains that the gulf between opera and lieder is now far wider than it was in the early 1950s, when the young Fischer-Dieskau ushered in a new age of lieder interpretation.

On the one hand we see glamour, stars and the masses and on the other high art, intellectuals and elitist programmes: stage spectacular versus special interest. As a result concert promoters have largely lost interest in song recitals over the last twenty years, preferring to leave the risk of organizing them to major festivals, where song recitals help to set the tone even if they generate relatively little income at the box office.

It is regularly argued that the music lovers who attend song recitals are far better educated than your average opera-goer. Remarks like Matthias Goerne's seem to confirm this impression: 'Whenever I give a lieder recital at the Wigmore Hall, I have the feeling that some of the listeners know these songs better than I do.' London's Wigmore Hall is the beating heart of lieder singing in England, while in Europe the Mecca of all lovers of lieder lies far from the hectic pace of life in the continent's capitals but is located some twenty minutes by car from the Austrian side of Lake Constance: in Hohenems and Schwarzenberg. The Schubertiade Festival was founded by Hermann Prey in 1976 and every year since then has featured the foremost lieder singers of our day. Here, too, it is clear that many in the audience know the repertory like the back of their hand. They come here primarily for the music and only secondarily for the singers. They have no need of the enchanted world of opera but want music in its purest form, above all in the guise of lieder and chamber music.

But for many singers this pure form seems to represent a hurdle, and this is especially true of those who are described as 'stage animals'. Whenever they assume a role and are able to hide behind costume and make-up they give their all, but as soon as these elements are lacking, they feel naked and vulnerable. On top of everything else, in songs they are singularly responsible for all that happens. They have no excuse if there is no atmosphere, and they have no conductor, no director, no designer to blame if they are prevented from giving a better and more beautiful performance. Nor can the pianist be blamed, since he or she was chosen by the singer. Although most of the classical lieder repertory places as many demands on the pianist as on the singer, it is mostly the singer who is the focus of interest. He is the narrator. And it is not a single story that he is telling but between twenty and thirty different stories in the course of a single evening, some of them familiar, others unknown. Every time they have to be able to create a specific atmosphere within a matter of seconds, immersing themselves in the emotional world of the composer and poet, recapturing the period at which the song was written and reimagining the situation for a listener who has not heard these songs before. But for many singers this is precisely where the appeal of lieder singing is to be found.

What drives a 'stage animal' like Jonas Kaufmann to sing lieder? Without belittling the challenges of the opera house and the concert hall, I think that performing lieder is the ne plus ultra of singing – initially on account of the particular situation here: together with the pianist, the singer is responsible for the entire event. And in choosing the programme he is largely free from outside influence. It is no longer necessary to keep making compromises but is easier to realize yourself as an artist. On the other hand, you have to maintain the same degree of tension all evening, from the very first minute to the last. And then there are the vocal demands: vocally and interpretatively, a full-length lieder recital is substantially more challenging than a normal operatic role. Every three or four minutes you have to relate to a different situation and assume a different persona. And the lieder repertory demands far more detailed work from the singer than any other vocal discipline: more colours, more nuances, more subtly differentiated dynamics and greater sophistication in your handling of the music and of the words.

If everything works, then a lieder recital can truly provide audiences with 'the magic of the moment'.

What do you mean by that?

That listeners no longer think about the artificiality of the art form but feel the poetry and music in its purest form. Take Mozart's song 'Das Veilchen' ('The Violet'): who nowadays gives a second thought to the fate of a poor violet that's been squashed flat? But anyone who hears this song sung by a great artist is bound to be moved by a subject that they might otherwise regard as trivial. This, for me, is the 'magic of the moment'. Quite apart from this, lieder recitals have a special dramaturgical appeal: you have an infinite number of possibilities of combining individual songs to create a particular story, you can range far and wide over different periods and styles and you can make connections between songs that in themselves have nothing to do with each other. Nor should you forget that every song tells its own self-contained story or, to take the example of Schubert's setting of Goethe's 'Erlkönig', that it constitutes a miniature drama in its own right. You have to be able to tell this story with music and words alone, without stage sets, without a costume and without make-up. These are the special challenges which in my view support the assertion that there is no other kind of singing that is as multi-layered and as demanding as lieder singing.

Mentor and partner: Helmut Deutsch

You've been giving song recitals since 2000, and with few exceptions your pianist has been Helmut Deutsch. Would it be true to say that it was he who introduced you to lieder singing?

Absolutely! He was one of my teachers at college, and it was he who opened my eyes and ears to lieder singing. Before I met him, I'd thought of lieder singing as something artificial. I'd always had the feeling that for the lieder repertory you needed to cultivate a different type of voice from the one used in opera. Broadly speaking: delicacy in lieder, belting in opera. In part this is true, but only in part. Before I met Helmut Deutsch, I almost always crooned when singing lieder. But then I had a seminal experience: I had a class with him and hadn't prepared for it. Also, my accompanist wasn't able to come that day. So I apologized and said: 'Sorry, I haven't prepared the songs. I've got an audition tomorrow, I'm already incredibly nervous and so I've practised only these arias.' – 'Well, let's practise the arias and then we'll at least have put the lesson to good use.' After a while Deutsch looked at me and said: 'Tell me, what kind of a voice are you using? Why do you never sing like that with me? The way you sang these arias is completely different from anything you've shown me when singing lieder.' And at that moment the penny dropped: lieder shouldn't be sung in an 'artificial' way but with your whole body and soul – not just with your head. 'Right,' Deutsch went on, 'now sing the songs that we practised last week, but this time let it all hang out.' And suddenly it worked. I'd previously been unable to impress anyone with my lieder singing because I mostly refused to let me voice flow freely. So this lesson with Deutsch was the start of my career as a lieder singer.

A masterclass with Hans Hotter

Shortly afterwards you were able to attend one of Hans Hotter's masterclasses.
It was at the Richard Strauss Festival in Garmisch. Helmut Deutsch took along five of his students. The fact that the women received more attention than the men was no doubt

just in the nature of things. Hotter was an old smoothy. Still fresh from the realization that lieder singing isn't the same as crooning, I threw caution to the winds. And the songs were by Strauss, so you can really let go. But Hotter keep interrupting me: 'Too loud! Too loud! Don't bellow like that, it's a quiet song. And for God's sake don't widen your tone, we're not trying to build ourselves a house here.' And so it went on, and of course it started to get to me. I'd finally discovered that in lieder singing, too, you have to come out of your shell – and now I was having to curl up again and hide. Also, Strauss most certainly didn't want this – even if a lieder singer as legendary as Hans Hotter says otherwise, a singer, moreover, who worked a lot with Strauss. So I didn't allow myself to get worked up but simply put up with it.

And how did Hotter react?

Well, he kept calling me to heel, which I really didn't like. I was correspondingly sceptical towards him. For his sake I sang a lot in a much more restrained way, but at the final concert – after first consulting Helmut – I once again put my foot on the gas. In spite of this I learnt a lot from Hotter's explanations, even though it was only much later that I was able to put a number of his suggestions into practice. His way of handling the language, which ideally combines sonority and words, is something that I was able to achieve only through relaxed singing devoid of any pressure. At that point linguistic intelligibility comes entirely naturally, and at the same time one can shape the phrases on the spur of the moment. I'm comforted by my view that he himself didn't sing in the way he later demanded as a teacher. In the booklet accompanying one of his recordings of *Winterreise* he wrote that it is not at all in the spirit of Schubert for the singer to imagine himself onstage passing through the different stages of this winter's journey. Rather, the singer should from start to finish maintain his persona as a neutral narrator. But in my own view Hotter is anything but neutral in this recording, and it is very much this that makes his interpretation so fascinating. This leads us on to a central question that all lieder and oratorio singers must ask themselves: is what the 'lyric self' is narrating felt and experienced at that very moment or does it lie in the past and is now being recounted from a safe distance, as it were? This is a question that begins with the Evangelist in Bach's Passions. I simply cannot imagine that this long and anguished phrase 'and wept bitterly' can be sung with a sense of distance as if it is being reported. Nor can I imagine singing Schubert's great song cycles from the perspective of a neutral narrator.

Schubert's Die schöne Müllerin *and* Winterreise

If forced to choose which of Schubert's three great song cycles they would record, most singers would presumably choose Winterreise. *But in 2009 you opted for* Die schöne Müllerin. *Why?*
I'd turned forty just a few weeks before the recording and I was keen to record this cycle before I became too old for it. Together with Schumann's *Dichterliebe*, *Die schöne Müllerin* is the song cycle that most demands a young voice – and also a young soul. After all, it's about a young man who is utterly carefree when he first heads out into the world but who then runs head-first into trouble. His unrequited love for the miller's daughter is his first experience of pain. In order for this 'innocence' to seem at all credible, the interpreter shouldn't sound too mature.

Both Winterreise *and* Die schöne Müllerin *end tragically. But what are the basic differences between these two cycles?*
In the case of *Winterreise* the basic tone of depression is present from the outset. You can hear at the start how the story will

end. This is something you must avoid at all costs in the case of *Die schöne Müllerin*.

But there have been significant interpreters who even in the first few songs of Die schöne Müllerin *have already hinted at the tragic ending and from the outset conveyed the feeling that this idyll is deceptive and disaster inevitable.*

I don't think that's right. To my mind the early songs are the purest expression of the boy's love of life, and that's how they should be performed. As he sets out on his wanderings, the boy is bursting with energy and self-confidence. The more successful you are in conveying this mood, the greater the fall and the bigger the gulf. That's also why I don't agree with people when they say that Wilhelm Müller's poems are just texts that Schubert has 'improved' with his music. I believe that Schubert fully recognized that the apparent simplicity of the poems serves to increase the sense of distance that is travelled and to heighten the sense of dislocation between the beginning and the end.

A test for any singer is the final lines of the fourteenth song, 'Der Jäger' ('The Huntsman'). Here the lad expresses his anger at his rival in what almost amounts to a scream. Is it legitimate in such extreme passages to switch to Sprechgesang?

The way that Schubert has notated it, the notation takes second place to the expression, and by the line 'Die Eber, die schieße, du Jägerheld!' ('Shoot the wild boar, you huntsman hero!'), the singer is knocked off course. Just as the miller's lad screams out his anger here, so the vocal line is disrupted. It's fine if you can concentrate on the score and sing this passage exactly as it's written, but I doubt if this is in the spirit of the composer. Naturalistic bellowing isn't a solution here either, of course. It is above all these borderline cases between singing and speaking that need to be phrased with particular skill.

Does the man throw himself in the brook and drown? Or does this happen only in his imagination?

The tremendous meditative darkness of this final song makes me think that there is a body in the water. Yes, I do think that he takes his own life. In the penultimate song, the dialogue between the miller lad and the brook, the boy thinks: 'Ah, down there, down there lies cool repose!' And in the final song, it is only the brook that speaks: 'Rest well! Rest well! Close your eyes! Weary wanderer, you are home. [...] I shall bed you down on a cool soft pillow.'

You spent the 2013–14 season focusing on Winterreise, *recording the cycle and singing it in ten European towns and cities. How would you explain to a novice what this cycle is all about?*

Winterreise is the story of a young man driven to despair by unrequited love. It all starts out well enough – 'The young woman spoke of love, her mother even of marriage' – but at some point the two of them clearly break up, or at least he leaves his 'sweetheart' at dead of night. And the greater the distance that he puts between them, the more he grows apart from life. Whether or not he consciously seeks death may be left an open question. He is, as he says, 'fatally wounded' and ultimately he sees only pain and death in all that he encounters in the world of nature. This longing for death is a constant theme in the cycle, and for this reason, if for no other, listeners who have not previously heard *Winterreise* should familiarize themselves with its content in advance. Schubert's friends were really quite shocked when they heard these songs for the first time. Given all the terrible news that nowadays rains down on us from every quarter, we ourselves tend be more callous than Schubert's contemporaries – but the cycle can really get to you, even today's listeners. Even we performers get sucked in by these songs each time we sing them, even though we know what to expect.

How is it that this song cycle is more popular with audiences than any other?

Perhaps their enthusiasm has to do with the work's cathartic impact. It has an almost meditative effect on me personally because Schubert expressed these emotional and psychological depths with a clarity and a simplicity that I find ultimately consoling, and this allows me to find my own inner balance.

How does the wanderer's story end? With suicide – as in the case of the miller's apprentice in Die schöne Müllerin? *In that case the organ-grinder in the final song would be the Grim Reaper.*

Helmut Deutsch doesn't think that *Winterreise* ends on the same note of tragedy as *Die schöne Müllerin*. In spite of the wanderer's pain and anger, there is in Helmut's view a sense of hope that he believes is expressed in the title of one of the last songs, 'Letzte Hoffnung' ('Last Hope'). Helmut also cites the passage where the wanderer says: 'Will kein Gott auf Erden sein, / sind wir selber Götter!' ('If there's no god on earth, then we ourselves are gods'). According to Helmut, no one would say this if he were about to kill himself. I see it differently. To my mind, 'Last Hope' is called this because the wanderer's last hope fades. And when he says 'then we ourselves are gods', I don't think that this means that he is pulling himself together to face life but that he is taking control of his life and, with it, the end of that life. In other words: 'If no god will take pity on me and allow me to freeze to death, then I myself shall have to put an end to my life, then I myself shall be God.' But it is also clear to him that, according to the laws of the Catholic Church, a man who takes his own life may not be buried in a churchyard. Hence the rhetorical question: 'Sind denn in diesem Hause die Kammern all besetzt?' ('Are all the chambers in this house occupied?') I also see the organ-grinder not as a potential travelling companion but as a figure in his imagination: like a madman talking to the ghost of a dead person. So I don't think that at the end the wanderer encounters a companion in misfortune.

Does the cycle contain something like a turning point, when despair is transformed into a farewell to life?
For me, it's the song 'Der greise Kopf' ('The Grey Head'). Here the wanderer sees and feels himself to be an old man. But the thought that he still has many years ahead of him leaves him profoundly depressed, which is why he decides to turn his back on society and to take his leave of life and of this world.

There have been repeated attempts to stage Winterreise. *Would something like that appeal to you?*
Only to a limited extent, for no production can ever be as multi-layered as the images and associations that the words and music trigger in the listener. Or, to put it another way: wouldn't a staged version fix the meaning of *Winterreise* and limit the listener's imagination?

Your recording of Winterreise *was well received and garnered a number of awards. At the same time, however, there were some strikingly harsh criticisms of it.* Winterreise *polarized opinion more than any other of your previous albums. How do you explain this?*
I think that with lieder singing and, more especially, the three Schubert song cycles, listeners' habits and expectations are even more fixed than they are in the case of my operatic roles. I know this very well from my college days. There was a very precise idea of what a singer had to sound like when singing Schubert. I assume that this image was influenced above all by the recordings of Dietrich Fischer-Dieskau, Hermann Prey and Peter Schreier. Anyone who deviates from this line inevitably causes puzzlement and annoyance for many listeners. And there

haven't been all that many instances of someone who sings Siegmund, Alvaro and Werther in the opera house also performing *Winterreise*. In recent years it tends to have been light lyrical voices like that of Ian Bostridge who have influenced responses to Schubert. If Jürgen Kesting says that my recording of *Winterreise* strikes him as a 'hand-me-down interpretation', I find it difficult to understand what he means because my voice allows and, indeed, obliges me to take a different approach from that of the great interpreters of the last fifty years. Also, every recording, whether live or studio-based, is a snapshot in time. It can show only the singer's current vocal state, not his artistic development – one is even more conscious of this with *Winterreise* than with any other work. That's undoubtedly one of the reasons why the great lieder singers have recorded this cycle more than once. Dietrich Fischer-Dieskau, for example, recorded at least one version during each decade of his professional life.

Any interpretation of Winterreise *is evidently a constant work in progress.*
Helmut and I noticed this very clearly when we took the work on tour six months after having recorded it. It was an exciting creative process. We approached these songs as if we were rediscovering them afresh each time. Of course, this kind of spontaneity works only with a partner whom you've known for years. And at best it can be documented in the form of live recordings of several performances, including comparisons and commentaries. This amounts to a kind of reportage that has nothing to do with the form of a classic recording.

You studied maths before switching to singing and in terms of vocal technique you're more of a physicist than a metaphysician, and in life you're a rationalist rather than a romantic. What does a person like you, who is normally guided by reason, feel when confronted by the emotional and psychological depths of Schubert's world?

I find that immersing myself in a completely different world provides me with a welcome sense of balance and, as a result, is a source of great happiness. There is so much about our profession – voice training, staying well, planning a career – than has to be guided by reason, just like the day-to-day life of any top athlete. But when I stand onstage in the evening and slip into a role, then every kind of rationality disappears. I then immerse myself in this alternative world to such an extent that I feel I am this other person and that they are my feelings and my situation. I doubt if *Winterreise* is much different from an operatic role in this regard. I know that in this context people repeatedly ask if lieder singing isn't more about objective observation and reporting than subjective emotion and fellow feeling. This may be true of a number of pieces, but as far as Schubert is concerned, I remain convinced that objective reporting is simply impossible. Anyone who claims to be able to sing this objectively is deluding himself.

Helmut Deutsch: 'Don't ever bring me anyone like that again!'

I can still recall our first meeting. It was in 1991, at the auditions for my lieder class at the Munich College of Music. Jonas sang 'Ich grolle nicht' ('I bear no grudge') from Schumann's *Dichterliebe* but in a key and in an edition I'd never seen before, namely a third higher than the normal version for high voice, so that at the dramatic outburst at the words 'und sah die Nacht in deines Herzens Raume' ('and saw the night within your heart') he sang a top C. That in itself was imposing and impressive, although his voice was then far lighter and more lyrical than it is now.

However well I can still recall this audition, I remember little about his first two years of study or, at least, I cannot really see him before me in the classroom. It may sound strange today, but although I thought he was a good singer, I never took him particularly seriously at that time. Jonas struck me as a young man with lots of interests and as someone astonishingly well versed in the most disparate subjects. You could talk to him about the latest developments in audio technology, he knew everything about mobile phones and computers, about wines and recipes and lots more besides. You got the impression that music and singing were among several things that interested him but that they were not necessarily his central concern.

In 1993 we spent two weeks in Tuscany with a group of students. We gave a handful of concerts in the area, including one in the piazza of a little provincial town, and I remember very clearly that Jonas was the only person to approach these concerts in a completely relaxed way – just as an evening's entertainment for a few tourists and nothing more. From my point of view he has retained this sense of composure and relaxation to a quite astonishing degree, no matter how significant the venue may be: when he started out, it was the Banqueting Hall in Bad Urach and the Town Hall in Heidelberg, whereas nowadays it is the Philharmonie in Berlin, Carnegie Hall and La Scala, Milan. I've never known Jonas to be nervous. Both on the podium and in private he remains relaxed and fully concentrated, with a healthy dose of self-awareness, but without ever becoming arrogant. And he is humorous, charming and genuinely committed to the subjects that particularly interest him.

As I was becoming increasingly convinced of Jonas's gifts, I introduced him to Christian Lange, who for many years had been Hermann Prey's personal assistant. Lange also ran the

Autumn Festival in Bad Urach, where Jonas finally gave his first concerts.

Although we never entirely lost sight of one another, there was a five-year period when we had nothing to do with each other musically. We started to give more substantial lieder recitals in 2001, when I proposed Jonas's name for the Summer Music Festival in Bad Kissingen. After the concert the intendant said to me: 'Don't ever bring me anyone like that again!' (She may now be regretting what she said on that occasion.) Only two months later Jonas enjoyed a major success at the Edinburgh Festival, where he was subsequently invited back to give annual lieder recitals. His voice and technique had developed enormously in the meantime, and even then it was already clear that he had the potential to become a truly great singer.

Of course, Jonas isn't the only student of mine whom I later met as a mature and experienced singer. Such meetings are always a little awkward, as there is a transitional period during which the relationship has to be redefined, and it's sometimes not so straightforward either for the singer or for me. But with Jonas there was never a problem in this regard, presumably in part because we were already friends while he was still studying with me. And so I found it rather amusing when, completely out of the blue, he suddenly started to beat about the bush: 'Supposing I were to ... Could I possibly ask you whether ... Could one ...' It went on like this for a while before I finally said to him: 'Just stop being so polite!'

It's clear that after nearly fifty years in the profession, I'm seen by most singers as a teacher and as a mentor. And naturally I try to pass on my experience. But people need to ensure that the term 'mentor' doesn't become a euphemism for 'smartarse' and for someone who never stops lecturing you. More than once I've heard former students tell me not to lecture them. But there was never any danger of this with Jonas and me. Over the years we've given lots of lieder recitals together, and I can't think of a single instance when we really held opposing views and the result was a battle of wills. Whenever we discuss things, it's rarely about questions of interpretation but mostly about basics: which repertory we should perform at a particular time – questions like that. For example, I advised Jonas not to wait too long before recording *Die schöne Müllerin*, because his voice might then be too heavy for certain songs and particular passages. But I'd never dare advise him on matters of vocal technique. At most, I might say: 'I think this vowel is too darkly coloured, too Bavarian.' But even this is relatively rare since he has now lost almost all trace of his Bavarian accent.

Jonas is a singer who thinks a lot about what he is singing and who knows an incredible amount about singing. If you sound him out on a particular point, he'll deliver a twenty-minute lecture on the subject. You could say he's an intellectual singer who avoids showing off his intellect, so that listeners have the impression he is singing from his gut. But this is, of course, completely untrue. Head, body and soul are always in a state of perfect balance with him. Which is how it should be with professional singers.

What fascinates me anew each time we work together is this mixture of lyricism, warmth and metal. He can sing in a wonderfully soft and inward voice but also, when required, he can really let rip. He has these radiant top notes, which are not often demanded in lieder singing, but for the songs of Richard Strauss they are ideal. If the voice really blossoms at the top of its range, as it needs to do in 'Cäcilie' or 'Heimliche Aufforderung', then as the accompanist I'm naturally delighted. Another of his strengths is his phenomenal breath control: he often seems able to sing infinitely long phrases on a single breath – longer than I've known with any other singer. Sometimes I even say to him while we're rehearsing, 'For heaven's sake take a breath, I'm almost suffocating just listening to you.' But Jonas often says: 'It harder to breathe here than it is to sing the phrase on a single breath.' Of course, I've become very spoilt by him in this respect, too. And sometimes when I'm working with other singers and think it may be a healthy encouragement, I let drop the remark: 'Well, Jonas doesn't breathe here!' The effect of this is often quite miraculous.

And there's something else that sets him apart from many other singers: he never repeats himself but re-imagines everything anew each time he performs it. I have to admit that before our tour of *Winterreise* in the spring of 2014 I had certain misgivings: I was afraid that in the course of the many performances the tension would drain away. But my qualms proved to be wholly unjustified: there was absolutely no trace of any routine. Each time he threw himself into it heart and soul, and each time it was different. Friends who attended several performances said afterwards that on this occasion they had heard completely different facets and colours from the ones they had noticed only two or three days earlier.

As a result of his annual appearances in cities such as Munich and Vienna we have the unusual problem of having to keep on learning new works. After all, it's impossible to sing *Winterreise* or *Dichterliebe* every two or three years in the same venue. Although Jonas learns exceptionally quickly, his operatic engagements – for which he also has to learn new roles – often get in the way. My dream would be to spend an entire year giving only lieder recitals, without any operas. But I expect I'd then find myself having to deal with an untold number of angry opera fans.

We've known each other for twenty-six years and have been performing together for sixteen. That's a long time, and it would be entirely normal if there were occasional tensions and disagreements between us as in any other relationship. But there have been no such disagreements – at least not when we've been together. The only thing that sometimes annoys me is his way of dealing with awkward questions that require an immediate answer but which he puts off answering for days or even weeks. But as soon as we meet up again, everything is restored to an even keel. In all the years we've known one another, there has never been a note of irritation or discord. Everything is wonderfully harmonious.

Jonas is the only singer in my long career who has remained completely loyal to me. On the few occasions when he's performed with another pianist, there have either been practical reasons for this or – once or twice – Daniel Barenboim has invited him to appear in concert with him. But the difference in age between us – I'm nearly twenty-five years older than he is – means that, for better or worse, I shall one day be replaced. I find it very touching that Jonas has so far refused to discuss this and immediately changes the subject whenever I try to raise it. And so I hope that I may be permitted to spend a few more years working with him.

Inner balance

Career and family

When Wolfgang, the son of Christa Ludwig and Walter Berry, was once asked in his parents' presence, 'Where are Mummy and Daddy?', the one-year-old pointed to a photograph on the wall. He'd scarcely seen his parents but was growing up with his grandmother. For Ludwig and Berry this was the downside of what Ludwig herself described in the 1960s as their 'flourishing business as singers'. In the longer term it is hard to reconcile the nomadic life of international opera singers with a happy family life at home. At some point all singers have to decide whether to take the whole family with them on tour or whether one of the parents should remain at home with the children.

For Margarete Joswig and Jonas Kaufmann this decision became unavoidable following the birth of their third child. Margarete gave up her operatic career and restricted herself to the occasional concert, although since her stage comeback in Wiesbaden in 2016 she is once again singing opera with great success. But to have had to leave her children in their younger years with a nanny while rehearsing a new production in another city would have robbed her of all enjoyment in her work. Song recitals and concerts are easier to reconcile with family life since singers are rarely away from home for more than a couple of days at a time. But with the passage of time it became increasingly difficult for Margarete to maintain this creative freedom as she was completely tied to the house, not just as a mother and as a housewife but also as her husband's manager. She worked as his personal assistant, organizing travel, checking contracts, maintaining his schedule, overseeing the production of all of his CDs, DVDs and radio and television broadcasts, and taking charge of all of the details associated with each of his appearances, from tickets and backstage lists to post-concert receptions. As a general rule, she would usually have to put in an extra shift in the office once she had put the children to bed.

For four years Margarete and I shared this work. I focused on the press releases and public relations work, while also liaising with record labels and advertising partners. It quickly became clear to me just how much time it takes to manage the career of an international artist.

In early April 2014 Margarete and Jonas Kaufmann announced that they were separating. They declined to explain the reasons for their separation, and with few exceptions their desire for privacy has so far been respected.

Jonas, you have always been very protective of your private life: no coverage of your home life in the press and no family documentaries on television. Your children were to have as normal an upbringing as possible. We agree that the story of your marriage was a private one, but as far as Margarete is concerned, we cannot simply ignore the part that she has played in your career. Nor would I want to do so. Anyone who knows us is aware of what I owe her and how important was her contribution to my success. She was the confidante that every artist desires. No one knows my voice as well as Margarete and no one has been as honest in telling me the truth. The number of people who are candid with you after a performance gets smaller the higher up the career ladder you are. Most people usually just nod and say, 'You were marvellous! Magnificent!' That's not something I can take seriously. So I'm all the more appreciative of Margarete's incorruptibility.

Looking back on it all now, would you say that it's unfortunately impossible to have both an international career and a happy family life?
Hmmm... There have been instances where this has worked, and even with us there were long periods when all was well, albeit only with considerable effort. It's just that I can't be both on the road and a father. Margarete was effectively a single parent for fifteen years. Of course, I tried to be at home as often as possible, and thanks to the offers that I received from the Bavarian State Opera and the Salzburg Festival, this worked for relatively long periods of time – but the itinerant life of an opera singer isn't particularly conducive to a family life. This often got me down while I was away, and I can still remember how much it pained me each time I returned home and my children's first question was: 'When do you have to leave again?' But what can you do?

Living out of a suitcase

There are singers who travel only with their families and who send their children to American schools while they are working in the United States.
We've sometimes done this ourselves whenever we've spent more than two months in New York. But this was exceptional, and I hope it remains the exception. Everyone knows how important it is for a child to have a home. Colleagues have sometimes said to me: 'Just take them with you. It will work if you've got a nanny and a private tutor. The main thing is that the children are with their parents.' But I think that this solution really only helps you as the parent as it salves your guilty

conscience. Your home can't be the centre of your professional life as you're away for most of the time. And so you look for solutions like this. But ultimately it's just a pretence.

It's not easy to deal with separation.
The fact that you can nowadays remain in contact by Skype really only makes it harder and more painful, because you can then see what you're missing. And if you've no friends or kind colleagues around you, you may fall into a deep well of depression.

What can help in a situation like that?
In the theatre I throw myself into my work, and that generally helps. It's harder when you're in your hotel room. Then I normally deal with the things that I never get round to doing at home – and I catch myself counting the days until I'm due to fly back home.

You've said that the role of a father is a continuous learning process.
Because you're constantly having a mirror held up to you and you can't pretend, not even to yourself. To that extent it's the same kind of corrective as the honesty that a tiny handful of people show when telling you the unvarnished truth after a performance. I don't want my children to respect me simply because I've achieved something special but because I'm their father. I first had to learn that you can't keep returning home from your travels and trying to catch up with their education and attempting to do things that you might have done if you'd been at home. That's pointless and senseless. But I can't help recalling the important stages that I've missed in my children's lives. When my daughter was confirmed, I suddenly realized how quickly time passes. Far too quickly.

How do your children respond to singing and classical music?
Very well. We've tried, of course, to get them to like classical music but we've never forced them in this direction. This should come about naturally. Whenever we're in the car together, they mostly play the latest playlist, which at least allows me to get to know the current hits. As for opera and classical music, we've always tried to adopt a relaxed approach at home. If they've been interested, we've taken them to the theatre. That's what happened in 2011, when I was rehearsing *Die Walküre* at the Met. All three of them were really interested and sang the leitmotifs to one another. Of course, tastes change over time. When my daughter was twelve or thirteen, she went through a phase of wanting nothing to do with classical music, but now she goes to the opera on a regular basis and is really enthusiastic about it. My middle son plays the piano very well and has a beautiful treble voice. He's shown astonishing self-assurance when singing at school performances. We'll have to wait and see with the youngest boy. At present he gets more fun out of Lego and Scalextric.

Tomorrow's audiences

As a singer you take very seriously the subject of opera and children and as a Campus Ambassador you have devoted a considerable amount of time and energy to the Bavarian State Opera's Young Audience Programme.
This is the result not only of my own experiences as a young boy at the opera but also with an eye to the audiences of tomorrow. Programmes such as Campus are the basis on which to educate the next generation of listeners and spectators as well as musicians and singers. I myself am a good example of where a performance for children can lead. Opera became my passion and then my profession, and so I have every reason to be

grateful to the German operatic system in general and to the Bavarian State Opera in particular. This is the least I can do to ensure that the children of today have a similar experience to the one that I myself enjoyed almost forty years ago.

Are performances of operas like the abridged version of Die Zauberflöte *that has been adapted to suit an audience of children not ultimately a trivialization of the original and, hence, an insult to a child's intelligence?*
Of course, children can easily feel that they're being taken for a ride if you try too hard. Most children are extremely sensitive to what is genuine and what isn't. But if the project is well conceived, as in the German CDs *Holzwurm der Oper* (*Woodworm of Opera*), and if performances for children are arranged and given by young people, then this can have an even more powerful impact on children than any normal performance, because it is then a shared experience for people of the same age. This was something we could all feel very clearly with *Nepomuk's Night*, the Campus version of Purcell's *The Fairy Queen*. There was a palpable sense of enthusiasm among the children in the audience, making me think that if they all became opera buffs, I wouldn't have to worry any longer about tomorrow's audiences.

So when people ask you about the future of opera, you can't simply dismiss them with reference to the old proverb that 'Creaking gates last longest'?
It's absolutely essential that we keep on asking ourselves what we can do to interest young people in opera and in classical music in general. The times when we could entrust this role to parents and schools are long since past. In schools, music and art lessons are being cut all the time, so we have to find other ways of introducing children and young people to classical music. Of course, there are some wonderful projects in many European towns and cities, but on a global level this is still far too little.

Do you think there's a chance of reaching a younger audience with cinema and outdoor broadcasts like the Bavarian State Opera's Opera for All relays during its annual summer festival?

Absolutely! People are unfortunately still afraid of entering these 'hallowed halls'. Even if there is no longer a strict dress code in opera houses today, the first thing that most people ask themselves if they've never been to the opera is 'What shall I wear? And what do I need to read in advance in order to be able to keep up with the conversation?' I've never heard cinema-goers ask this sort of question. Opera is clearly still regarded by many people as the preserve of the initiated from the educated middle classes. I certainly think that cinema relays and open-air broadcasts in public places can help to break down inhibitions. In short, I'm not just interested in winning over younger audiences but, more generally, in gaining a wider public for opera. I've made this my special cause in life because I think that opera is far too precious as an art form to be reduced to a luxury entertainment for the well-to-do. A good opera performance can be a life-changing experience, and it's not just artists who have discovered this for themselves; the same is true of the people who seek us out or write to us after a performance. A good opera has the power to move the masses.

Helene Fischer and John Malkovich

Anyone who strikes out in this general direction immediately incurs the wrath of the self-styled champions of 'high art'. 'Do you really have to tarnish your reputation in this way?' Hermann Prey and Anneliese Rothenberger regularly had to put up with reproaches of this kind whenever they appeared on television shows. And a number of viewers reacted in the same way when you yourself appeared on the Helene Fischer Show.

Yes, this is first and foremost a German phenomenon: an opera singer has only to appear on a popular show for a group to emerge from the woodwork warning against the trivialization of the artistic content. Some people find this sort of appearance simply 'unworthy of a serious artist'. I think it's fairly arrogant of them to take this position, especially towards those viewers who aren't 'members of the circle of initiates'. These appearances are regarded as less questionable in the United States and Great Britain than they are in Germany, perhaps because English-speaking audiences don't draw such a strict distinction between serious music and pop music. When Birgit Nilsson sang 'Wien, Wien, nur du allein' ('Vienna, City of My Dreams') on an American television show, people thought it was great to hear the leading Brünnhilde and Turandot of her generation performing a completely different kind of repertory. Or take the legendary Last Night of the Proms in London's Albert Hall. It's a great show made up of the most varied musical numbers – and if a well-known opera singer performs there, it's certainly not thought of as questionable but is a huge honour and a great distinction.

You yourself were the vocal soloist at the Last Night on 12 September 2015 – and the first German in the history of these concerts to sing 'Rule, Britannia!'.
It was one big party both inside the Albert Hall and outside in Hyde Park. I thought that it was tremendous fun. I continue to be fascinated by the way in which the masses can be moved by a programme of classical music. And when I see that I can reach an audience of millions with tenor hits by Puccini and Lehár, then I've absolutely no reason to feel ashamed. And when some people claim that it demonstrates a lack of seriousness to sing Lehár alongside Schubert, Brahms and Beethoven, I can only respond by saying that even Richard Tauber had to put up with the criticism that he'd demeaned himself by singing

in operettas. I love operetta in all of its variety, from the senti-
mental to the saucy, from the classical to the satirical, and I'd
very much like to play my part in making sure that this art
form once again receives the respect that it deserves. By the
same token, the cinema hits that were written for great singers
such as Tauber, Joseph Schmidt and Jan Kiepura should find
a wider audience again. I also find it tremendous fun to sing
this repertory. And with the exception of the above-mentioned
prophecies of doom, our project *Du bist die Welt für mich* was
greeted entirely positively.

*Can you say something about the background to your first cinema
film,* The Casanova Variations, *with John Malkovich?*
I'd said in the course of an interview that I'd like to appear in
a film but as an actor, rather than as a singer. And in answer
to the question as to what I was currently reading, I said
'Casanova's diaries'. The director Michael Sturminger heard
about this while he was filming his play about Casanova and so
he immediately offered me a small part in the film. Fortunately
I was able to clear my schedule and make myself available for a
couple of days, during which time I flew to Lisbon and filmed
a scene with John Malkovich. In it I play a rival of Casanova's
whom he injures in a duel.

*And on this occasion you sing a bass-baritone role, taking Don
Alfonso's line in the trio 'Soave sia il vento' from* Così fan tutte.
We recorded it live in the Teatro Nacional de São Carlos
with innumerable cameras. In the play Mozart's music is, so
to speak, the complementary colour to the text of Casanova's
diaries. Sturminger created some fascinating parallels. And
John Malkovich was overjoyed to be finally making a film with
classical music. He's a great music lover. As a child he dreamt of
joining the Vienna Boys' Choir.

'A completely normal person'

Speaking of the Vienna Boys' Choir, what would be your first piece of advice to a young singer?
Learn to make music with your voice in the same way that a musician does on his or her instrument. Acquire a solid technique that allows you to express everything that you can envisage in your imagination. Plan your work not according to the competition but follow your own path unwaveringly. Find your own voice and your own very personal way of communicating with other people by means of your voice. And never forget why you decided to pursue this particular course in life: out of a love of art, a love of music and a desire to reach out to people and move them with your singing.

Time and again it's said that you're a 'completely normal person' – and I have the impression that you, too, are keen to remain just that.
I'd find it very disagreeable if people were to say that success had gone to my head, since it's not true. Or at least I don't think it is. In any case, I haven't forgotten how much I had to struggle during the early part of my professional life. And it's clear to me that in every generation there are singers who have it in them to enjoy a major career but who for whatever reason fail to achieve their goal. I myself was often helped by favourable circumstances. I had a lot of good luck and have every reason to feel grateful for that. To say that I owe it all to my own hard work would be arrogant.

Is it true that you find it difficult to accept a compliment?
It depends. If someone tells me after a performance that they were particularly moved by a particular scene or if members of the chorus write to me after the last performance and say

'Please don't go', then that naturally pleases me a lot. But if someone gushes over me and won't stop or if I'm wooed and worshipped, then I find it embarrassing and have difficulty dealing with it.

It's relatively easy to defuse a situation like that, as the actress Elisabeth Flickenschildt once did when she was out shopping. A young girl rushed up to her and asked in a quivering voice: 'Sorry, but aren't you Elisabeth Flickenschildt?' To which the actress replied whispering: 'Yes, I am indeed, my dear child! Isn't that absolutely *wonderful?'*

Well, she could afford to do that. I'm not sure I'd have so much chutzpah, though a healthy assessment of one's own abilities is certainly a part of it. If you want to radiate a certain charisma or if you have to play a part that screams 'Look at me!', you can't go out onstage with a hangdog look. I spent a long time struggling with self-doubt and had to hide my insecurity, which sometimes came across as arrogance. With time I overcame this, as, indeed, I had to. The higher you climb, the thinner the air and the greater the pressure. Everyone expects an unforgettable performance, but no singer can give fifty unforgettable performances a year. And if your voice cracks on a note, you can be sure that two hours later that particular passage will be posted on YouTube. You need plenty of self-confidence to deal with pressures like that.

What are the character traits and kinds of behaviour that you value most?
Honesty. Loyalty. Naturalness. When someone is defined not by their professional success but by their humanity. I've no time for a diva's airs and graces and I also have problems with people who claim to be better than they are.

What makes you really annoyed?
Injustice, malicious gossip and meanness. People who are always testing your limits and whom you have to keep on showing that they can go only up to a certain point and no further. Double standards. And when artists are judged by their market value rather than by their abilities. It annoyed me, for example, when certain companies took the view, 'Let's wait and see if he's successful at the Met before we offer him anything.'

Comparisons and models

How do you react to comparisons with other singers?
It depends on whether it's flattering or not (*laughs*). Yes, of course I'm pleased if I'm mentioned in the same breath as Plácido Domingo, Franco Corelli, Jon Vickers and Fritz Wunderlich and if people see me, as it were, as continuing this great tradition. And I'm fond of drawing comparisons myself – not along the lines of 'Who's the best, the most beautiful, the greatest?' but because I love to hear very different interpretations of the same role. Nicolai Gedda and Fritz Wunderlich, for example. Both were great singers, both of them inspired me, and yet they were completely different in terms of their voices and interpretation. Here it would be idiotic to play off one of them against the other. Gedda sang in every language and every style, whether lyric or dramatic. There was nothing he couldn't do. And his voice remained flexible and round. And this effortlessness! When you listen to his recording of *Benvenuto Cellini*, for example, you think: 'Oh, that's easy enough.' But when I look at the score, I think it's ridiculous. Fritz Wunderlich sang everything with such love and hope, such passion and fire that it made you think it was the last performance he was ever going to give. Whenever he sang, he was not just one hundred per cent an artist but one hundred

per cent a human being: there was always a direct link between his feelings and those of his listeners. With him, even insipid music and impossible words sounded like the most beautiful thing in the world. I'll be taking his recording of 'Granada' with me to my desert island. His singing is incredible, absolutely bursting with energy. Or take *Das Lied von der Erde*: the sense of ecstasy in 'Das Trinklied vom Jammer der Erde' is simply insane. To be able to thrill an audience in the way that Wunderlich was always able to do – that would be quite something.

What do you feel about the constant comparison with Plácido Domingo?
I take it as a great compliment. I admire him for his energy and his tremendous achievements. He's the absolute exception to every rule. My own defining experience with him was a performance of *Parsifal* in Bayreuth. Whenever he appeared onstage, it was as if a film had suddenly switched from black and white to colour. This was the first time that I'd realized what stage presence and charisma can mean in concrete terms.

Unlike many singers, who, while studying a new role, go out of their way to avoid any kind of 'influence', you listen to recordings by your predecessors when you're preparing a new part.
Yes, but, if possible, not by singers whom I admire, because if I really like something, I run the risk of following in their footsteps and abandoning my own particular path, so I prefer to listen to recordings where I think: 'Well, I'll do that differently.' Or I listen to several very different recordings so that one particular reading doesn't get stuck in my mind.

Are there times when you wish you had some other singer's voice?
Not any more. But there have been times when I'd like to have sounded like Wunderlich or Corelli. And if you have a certain

talent for imitating others, you try to mimic the sound that you think is so great, but this is, of course, the quickest way to lose your own identity. Or, to put it more positively, there's nothing that you can do better as a singer than discover your own voice. This is ultimately what matters: you need to work out what makes you unique and treat your own voice as something that's unmistakably yours. I can still remember listening to the radio with my father and being amazed when he said: 'That's Hermann Prey.' How could he know that when there'd been no announcement? Since then I've always paid attention to what makes a voice unique. You really have to discover your very own sound, a sound that doesn't have to be the most beautiful in the world, just your own. I think that only then can you achieve what's known as 'singing with the soul'. Unfortunately, this is not really encouraged today. Most lessons are to do with technique. That's a good thing, of course, as I need a good technique to be able to sing for a long time. But where is the audience that just wants to hear technique? Certainly not me. Singers can rattle off their coloratura as quickly as they like, they can pirouette and produce a crescendo and a diminuendo three times on the most impossible notes, but if there is no soul to their singing, it leaves me cold. Conversely, there have been many great singers whose singing is so powerfully expressive that audiences never for a moment think about questions of technique.

Singing and the soul

'Soulful' is a word that few people dare use today.
Perhaps because it strikes most people as too kitschy. But when you're talking about singing, it's irreplaceable as a word, because it describes a state that you achieve not by sheer force of will but by letting things happen of their own accord, not as the result

of some effort or achievement but through simply 'being'. This is as fundamental to singing as it is to Zen archery. And singers shouldn't shy away from confronting these matters.

Could I then ask you the crunch question?
What's my attitude to religion? I believe in God, there are even times when I pray. Margarete and I have brought up our children to respect Christian values. I think we need these values today more than ever, so that what's left of our humanity doesn't descend into violence and chaos. The message of the Sermon on the Mount is at least as relevant today as it was two thousand years ago: stop the escalation of violence. I do, however, have a problem with the Church as an institution and prefer to stick to the Bible's message: 'For where two or three are gathered together in my name, there am I in the midst of them.'

Are you Catholic or Protestant?
Protestant. My parents didn't go to church but they lived their lives according to Christian and humanist values, and that left its mark on me. Also, the music of Johann Sebastian Bach has always impressed and exercised me. Even so, I've always had problems with the Protestant view of our lives here on earth. The belief that it's all just a way of preparing us for the afterlife, not to mention all of this self-accusation and self-mortification... From this point of view the hedonist in me has always envied Catholics, who are allowed to enjoy life far more than we are.

Is the subject of death taboo for you?
Not since the death of my father. He had an incredible love of life, he loved parties and loved having people around him. He died while I was rehearsing *Eine Nacht in Venedig* (*A Night in Venice*) in Regensburg. I was twenty-five then and it took me a long time to get over it. Since I have difficulty repressing my

emotions, I was forced to deal with his loss in an entirely conscious way. For example, I went trekking in the Tirol without a guide simply in order to be on my own with just my own thoughts as company. Since then death has lost its terrors for me. I'm not afraid of it. And now I know how important it is to find an inner balance, to be able to spend time on my own, to do yoga, to read books and watch films – or do nothing at all. Simply to unwind. I'm convinced that this has also had an impact on my singing. All of the emotions that you have to express onstage or at a song recital must ultimately be ones that you carry around inside you. 'The voice,' it is said, 'is the mirror of the soul.' That may sound a little pompous, but it really hits the nail on the head.

Appendix

Timeline

10 July 1969	Born in Munich
1989–91	Studies as an opera and concert singer at Munich's College of Music and Theatre
1993–94	Caramello in Johann Straus's *Eine Nacht in Venedig* in Regensburg
May 1994	Tamino in a concert performance of Mozart's *Die Zauberflöte* at Munich's Prinzregententheater
1994–96	First permanent engagement at the Saarbrücken State Theatre
April 1995	Bach's *St Matthew Passion*, at the Alte Oper in Frankfurt
1996	World premiere of Antonio Bibalo's *The Glass Menagerie* in Trier
1997	*Die Zauberflöte* in Würzburg; Romberg's *The Student Prince* at the Heidelberg Castle Festival; Szymanowski's *King Roger* in Stuttgart
1998	Mozart's *Così fan tutte* at the Piccolo Teatro in Milan; Jaquino (*Fidelio*) and Almaviva (*Il barbiere di Siviglia*) in Stuttgart

1999	Mozart's *La clemenza di Tito* in Klagenfurt; Salzburg Festival debut in Busoni's *Doktor Faust*
2000	*Così fan tutte* in Hamburg, Frankfurt and Wiesbaden; Alfredo (*La traviata*) in Stuttgart and Florestan in Paer's *Leonora* in Winterthur
2001	Wilhelm Meister (*Mignon*) in Toulouse; USA debut as Cassio (*Otello*) at the Lyric Opera of Chicago
2002	*Die Zauberflöte, Die Entführung aus dem Serail, Il ritorno d'Ulisse in patria* and Paisiello's *Nina* in Zurich; Berlioz's *La damnation de Faust* at La Monnaie in Brussels; recitals in Spoleto and Edinburgh; Florestan in concert performances of *Fidelio* at the Rheingau Music Festival, the Beethoven Festival in Bonn and in Stuttgart; Flamand (*Capriccio*) in Turin
2003	*La traviata* in Chicago; concerts in Tokyo; *La damnation de Faust* in Geneva; *Die Entführung aus dem Serail* and *La clemenza di Tito* at the Salzburg Festival; *Die Zauberflöte* at the Komische Oper in Berlin
2004	*Fidelio* and *Faust* in Zurich; Cassio (*Otello*) at the Opéra Bastille in Paris; *Der Freischütz* and *Capriccio* at the Edinburgh Festival; Covent Garden debut as Ruggero in Puccini's *La rondine*
2005	*Falstaff, Rigoletto, La clemenza di Tito, Così fan tutte* and Schubert's *Fierrabras* in Zurich; Beethoven's *Missa solemnis* in Cleveland; Humperdinck's *Königskinder* in Montpellier
2006	Metropolitan Opera debut as Alfredo (*La traviata*); Mahler's *Das Lied von der Erde* at the

Berlin Philharmonie; *Fierrabras* at the Châtelet in Paris; *Parsifal* in Zurich; *The Bartered Bride* in Frankfurt; *Die Zauberflöte* at the Vienna State Opera; concert performance of Wagner's *Die Meistersinger von Nürnberg* at the Edinburgh Festival; *Die Zauberflöte* at the Met; Don José (*Carmen*) in London

2007   *La traviata* in Zurich, at the Palais Garnier in Paris and at La Scala, Milan; *Königskinder* and *La bohème* in Zurich; first solo CDs (Strauss lieder and *Romantic Arias*)

2008   *La bohème* at the Berlin State Opera; *La traviata* in London and at the Met; *Carmen* in Zurich; *Tosca* in London; *Manon* in Chicago; *Fidelio* at the Palais Garnier

2009   CD of arias by Mozart, Schubert, Beethoven and Wagner; *Tosca* in Zurich and Vienna; *Manon* in Vienna; *Lohengrin* at the Munich Opera Festival; CD of *Die schöne Müllerin*; *Don Carlo* in London; the Verdi *Requiem* at the Salle Pleyel in Paris and at La Scala; opens new season at La Scala as Don José (*Carmen*)

2010   *Werther* at the Opéra Bastille; *Tosca* and *Carmen* at the Met and in Munich; Bayreuth debut in a new production of *Lohengrin*; *Fidelio* in Lucerne and Munich; Cilea's *Adriana Lecouvreur* at the Deutsche Oper in Berlin and at Covent Garden

2011   *Carmen* in Munich; *Tosca* at La Scala; Siegmund (*Die Walküre*), Faust and a solo recital at the Met; *Tosca* at Covent Garden; concert tour with Anna Netrebko and Erwin Schrott at the

Königsplatz in Munich, the Stadthalle in Vienna
and the Waldbühne in Berlin

2012   *Don Carlo* in Munich; *Faust* in Vienna;
concert tour with Andris Nelsons visiting
Symphony Hall in Birmingham, the Théâtre
des Champs-Élysées in Paris, the Philharmonie
in Munich and the Musikverein in Vienna;
Carmen, Ariadne auf Naxos and *La bohème*
at the Salzburg Festival; the Verdi *Requiem* in
Salzburg, at La Scala and in Lucerne; opens new
season at La Scala as Lohengrin

2013   *Parsifal* at the Met; Wagner CD; Wagner
concert at the Dresden State Opera; *Don Carlo*
in London and Munich and at the Salzburg
Festival; *La fanciulla del West* in Vienna; Verdi
CD; *Il trovatore* and *La forza del destino* in
Munich

2014   CD of *Winterreise*; *Werther* at the Met;
European tour with *Winterreise* and songs by
Mahler, Wagner and Strauss; *Du bist die Welt
für mich*; Puccini's *Manon Lescaut* in London
and Munich

2015   *Andrea Chénier* in London; double debut
in *Cavalleria rusticana* and *Pagliacci* at the
Salzburg Easter Festival; concert tour with
Du bist die Welt für mich; Japan tour (Osaka,
Kawasaki, Tokyo); concert with Anna Netrebko
on the Königsplatz in Munich; Puccini concert
at La Scala; *Carmen* in Orange; *Fidelio* at the
Salzburg Festival; *Aida* in Munich; soloist at the
Last Night of the Proms; Berlioz's *La damnation
de Faust* in Paris

2016   *Tosca* in Vienna and Munich; Walther (*Die Meistersinger von Nürnberg*) in Munich; all six movements of *Das Lied von der Erde* at the Musikverein in Vienna and at the Théâtre des Champs-Élysées in Paris; South American debut tour (Buenos Aires, São Paulo, Lima, Santiago de Chile).

2017   *Lohengrin* in Paris; recital and Act One of *Die Walküre* at the Barbican in London; *Andrea Chénier* in Munich; *Otello* (debut) at the Royal Opera House.

Awards (selection)

2007   *Gramophone* Award (Strauss lieder)

2008   Diapason d'or (*Romantic Arias*)
Singer of the Year (*Opernwelt*)

2009   GQ Man of the Year in the classical music category
Gramophone Award (*Madama Butterfly*)

2010   Echo Klassik Award as Singer of the Year (*Sehnsucht*)
Diapason d'or (*Verismo Arias*)

2011   Chevalier de l'Ordre des Arts et des Lettres
Gramophone Award (*Verismo Arias*)

2012   Vocalist of the Year (*Musical America* for *Verismo Arias*)
Medal for Special Services to Bavaria in a United Europe

2013   Recording of the Year (*Limelight* Magazine for Wagner album)

Singer of the Year and Readers' Award
(International Opera Awards)
Echo Klassik Award as Singer of the Year
(Wagner album)
Awarded the title of Bavarian Kammersänger
Gramophone Award (Wagner album)

2014   Golden Disc (Verdi album)
Echo Klassik Award for Solo Recording of the
Year (Verdi album)
Gramophone Award (*Winterreise*)
Bambi Award in the category of classical music

2015   Europäischer Kulturpreis; Echo Klassik Award
as Singer of the Year (*Du bist die Welt für mich*)

2016   Bundesverdienstkreuz (Federal Order of Merit);
Echo Klassik Award for the Bestseller of the
Year (Puccini album); Golden Disc (*Du bist die
Welt für mich*)

2017   Les Victoires de la Musique Classique

Discography

SOLO ALBUMS

Jonas Kaufmann (released in German-speaking countries as
Sehnsucht)
Scenes from operas by Mozart, Schubert, Beethoven
and Wagner; Kaufmann, Joswig, Volle, Mahler Chamber
Orchestra, Abbado; Decca (CD); 2009

Nessun dorma
Arias and scene from Puccini operas (*Manon Lescaut, Le
villi, Edgar, La bohème, Tosca, Madama Butterfly, La fanciulla
del West, La rondine, Il tabarro, Gianni Schicchi, Turandot*);

Kaufmann, Opolais, Orchestra and Chorus of the Accademia Nazionale di Santa Cecilia, Pappano; Sony (CD); 2014

Romantic Arias
Scenes from operas by Puccini, Bizet, Flotow, Verdi, Weber, Massenet, Gounod, Wagner, Berlioz; Kaufmann, Prague Philharmonic Orchestra, Armiliato; Decca (CD); 2007

The Verdi Album
Arias and scenes from *Rigoletto, Aida, Un ballo in maschera, Il trovatore, Luisa Miller, Simon Boccanegra, Don Carlo, La forza del destino, I masnadieri, Otello*; Kaufmann, Gregnanin, Grimaldi, Vassallo, Cusari, Orchestra dell'Opera di Parma, Morandi; Sony (CD); 2013

Verismo Arias
Arias and scenes from operas by Zandonai, Giordano, Cilea, Leoncavallo, Mascagni, Boito, Ponchielli, Refice; Kaufmann, Westbroek, Orchestra and Chorus of the Accademia Nazionale di Santa Cecilia, Pappano; Decca (CD); 2010

Wagner
Scenes and arias from *Die Walküre, Siegfried, Rienzi, Tannhäuser, Die Meistersinger von Nürnberg, Lohengrin*; *Wesendonck Lieder* (orch. Mottl); Kaufmann, Brück, Chorus and Orchestra of the Deutsche Oper Berlin, Runnicles; Decca (CD); 2012

Mahler, *Das Lied von der Erde*
Kaufmann, Vienna Philharmonic, Nott; Sony (CD); 2017

Schubert, *Die schöne Müllerin*
Kaufmann, Deutsch; Decca (CD); 2009

Schubert, *Winterreise*
Kaufmann, Deutsch; Sony (CD); 2013

Strauss, Lieder
Kaufmann, Deutsch; harmonia mundi (CD); 2006

Du bist die Welt für mich
Songs and arias from operettas by Lehár, Kálmán, Richard
Tauber, Benatzky, Abraham and Künneke; cinema hits by
Stolz, May, Heymann and Spoliansky; 'Glück, das mir verblieb'
by Korngold; Kaufmann, Kleiter, Berlin Radio Symphony
Orchestra, Rieder; Sony (CD); 2014

Dolce Vita
Italian songs by Dalla, Leoncavallo, Rota and others;
Kaufmann, Orchestra del Teatro Massimo di Palermo, Fisch;
Sony (CD and DVD); 2016

COMPLETE OPERAS

Abert, *Ekkehard*
Van Ingen, Kelling, Böhm, Hempel, Reiter, Gerhaher,
Kaufmann (Ekkehard), Fujimura; Stuttgarter Choristen,
SWR Radio Orchestra Kaiserslautern, Falk; Capriccio (2 CDs);
1998

Beethoven, *Fidelio*
Nylund, Kaufmann, Muff, Polgár, Magnuson, Strehl,
Groissböck and others, Chorus and Orchestra of the Zürich
Opera, Harnoncourt; director: Flimm; Arthaus (DVD); 2004

Stemme, Kaufmann, Struckmann, Fischesser, Harnisch, Strehl,
Mattei and others, Arnold Schoenberg Choir, Mahler Chamber
Orchestra/Lucerne Festival Orchestra, Abbado; Decca (2 CDs);
2010

Pieczonka, Kaufmann, Konieczny, König, Bezsmertna, Ernst,
Holecek and others, Vienna State Opera Chorus, Vienna
Philharmonic, Welser-Möst; director: Guth; Sony (DVD/Blu-
ray); Salzburg Festival 2015

Bizet, *Carmen*
Antonacci, Kaufmann, Amsellem, D'Arcangelo and others,
Chorus and Orchestra of the Royal Opera House, Pappano;
director: Zambello; Decca (DVD/Blu-ray); 2006

Kasarova, Kaufmann, Rey, Pertusi and others, Chorus and
Orchestra of the Zürich Opera, Welser-Möst; director:
Hartmann; Decca (DVD/Blu-ray); 2008

Kožená, Kaufmann, Kühmeier, Smoriginas and others, Chorus
of the Berlin State Opera, Berlin Philharmonic, Rattle; Warner
(2 CDs); 2012

Cilea, *Adriana Lecouvreur*
Gheorghiu, Kaufmann, Borodina, Corbelli and others, Chorus
and Orchestra of the Royal Opera House, Elder; director:
McVicar; Decca (DVD/Blu-ray); 2012

Giordano, *Andrea Chénier*
Kaufmann, Westbroek, Lučić and others, Chorus and
Orchestra of the Royal Opera House, Pappano; director:
McVicar; Warner Classics (DVD/Blu-ray); 2016

Gounod, *Faust*
Kaufmann, Poplavskaya, Pape and others, Metropolitan Opera
Orchestra, Chorus and Ballet, Nézet-Séguin; director: McNuff;
Decca (DVD/Blu-ray); 2011

Humperdinck, *Königskinder*
Sala, Kaufmann, Roth, Gubisch and others, Chœur de la
Radio Lettone, Orchestre National de Montpellier, Jordan;
Accord/Universal (3 CDs); 2005 (live)

Rey, Kaufmann, Widmer, Nikiteanu and others, Chorus and
Orchestra of the Zürich Opera, Metzmacher; director: Herzog;
Decca (DVD/Blu-ray); 2010

Leoncavallo, *Pagliacci*
Agresta, Kaufmann, Platanias, Akzeybek, Arduini, Dresden
State Opera Chorus and Dresden Staatskapelle, Thielemann;
director: Stölzl; Sony (DVD/Blu-ray); 2015 Salzburg Easter
Festival (issued with *Cavalleria rusticana*)

Loewe, *Die drei Wünsche*
Hawlata, Florian Prey, May, Klepper, Worner, Weber,
Kaufmann, Stuttgarter Choristen, SWR Radio Orchestra, Falk;
Capriccio (2 CDs); 1998

Marschner, *Der Vampyr*
Kaufmann, Hawlata, Klepper, Hoffmann, Marquardt and
others, Chorus and Orchestra of WDR Cologne, Froschauer;
Capriccio (2 CDs); 2001

Mascagni, *Cavalleria rusticana*
Monastyrska, Kaufmann, Toczyska, Maestri, Stroppa, Dresden
State Opera Chorus and Dresden Staatskapelle, Thielemann;
director: Stölzl; Sony (DVD/Blu-ray); 2015 Salzburg Easter
Festival (issued with *Pagliacci*)

Massenet, *Werther*
Kaufmann, Koch, Tézier and others, Chorus and Orchestra of
the Opéra national de Paris, Plasson; director: Jacquot; Decca
(DVD/Blu-ray); 2010

Monteverdi, *Il ritorno d'Ulisse in patria*
Henschel, Rey, Kasarova, Kaufmann, Scharinger and others,
Chorus and Orchestra of the Zürich Opera, Harnoncourt;
director: Grüber; Arthaus (DVD); 2002

Mozart, *La clemenza di Tito*
Kaufmann, Mei, Kasarova, Nikiteanu, Hartelius, Groissböck,
Chorus and Orchestra of the Zürich Opera, Welser-Möst;
director: Miller; EMI (DVD); 2005

Paisiello, *Nina, o sia La pazza per amore*
Bartoli, Kaufmann, Polgár and others, Chorus and Orchestra
of the Zürich Opera, Fischer; director: Lievi; Arthaus (DVD);
2002

Puccini, *Madama Butterfly*
Gheorghiu, Kaufmann, Shkosa, Capitanucci and others,
Chorus and Orchestra of the Accademia Nazionale de Santa
Cecilia, Pappano; EMI (2 CDs); 2008

Tosca
Magee, Kaufmann, Hampson and others, Chorus and
Orchestra of the Zürich Opera, Carignani; director: Carsen;
Decca (DVD); 2009

Gheorghiu, Kaufmann, Terfel and others, Chorus and
Orchestra of the Royal Opera House, Pappano; director: Kent;
Warner (DVD/Blu-ray); 2011

Schubert, *Fierrabras*
Polgár, Banse, Volle, Strehl, Groissböck, Kaufmann, Robinson
and others, Chorus and Orchestra of the Zürich Opera,
Welser-Möst; director: Guth; EMI (DVD); 2005

Strauss, *Der Rosenkavalier*
Fleming, Sophie Koch, Damrau, Hawlata, Grundheber,
Kaufmann, Vilsmeier and others, Munich Philharmonic,
Thielemann; director: Wernicke; Decca (DVD/Blu-ray); 2009
Baden-Baden Festival

Ariadne auf Naxos (Salzburg version)
Magee, Kaufmann, Moşuc, Obonya and others, Vienna
Philharmonic, Harding; director: Bechtolf; Sony (DVD/
Blu-ray); 2012

Verdi, *La forza del destino*
Harteros, Kaufmann, Tézier, Kowaljow, Krasteva and others,

Bavarian State Opera Chorus, Bavarian State Orchestra, Fisch;
director: Kušej; Sony (DVD/Blu-ray); 2014

Don Carlo
Kaufmann, Harteros, Salminen, Hampson, Semenchuk,
Halfvarson and others, Vienna State Opera Chorus, Vienna
Philharmonic, Pappano; director: Stein; Sony (DVD/Blu-ray);
2013

Aida
Harteros, Kaufmann, Semenchuk, Tézier, Schrott and others,
Chorus and Orchestra of the Accademia Nazionale di Santa
Cecilia, Pappano; Warner (2 CDs); 2015

Wagner, *Tannhäuser*
Seiffert, Kringelborn, Kabatu, Trekel, Muff, Kaufmann, Götzen
and others, Chorus and Orchestra of the Zürich Opera,
Welser-Möst; director: Herzog; EMI (DVD); 2003

Lohengrin
Kaufmann, Harteros, Schuster, Koch, Fischesser, Nikitin,
Bavarian State Opera Chorus, Bavarian State Orchestra,
Nagano; director: Jones; Decca (DVD/Blu-ray); 2009

Die Walküre
Voigt, Westbroek, Kaufmann, Terfel and others, Metropolitan
Opera Orchestra, Levine; director: Lepage; Deutsche
Grammophon (DVD/Blu-ray); 2011

Stemme, Kampe, Kaufmann, Pape, Mariinsky Orchestra,
Gergiev; Mariinsky (4 CDs); 2011

Parsifal
Kaufmann, Dalayman, Pape, Mattei, Nikitin and others,
Metropolitan Opera Orchestra, Chorus and Ballet, Gatti;
director: Girard; Sony (DVD/Blu-ray); 2013

Weber, *Oberon*
Davislim, Martinpelto, Comparato, Kaufmann, Dazeley and
others, Monteverdi Choir, Orchestre Révolutionnaire et
Romantique, Gardiner; Philips (2 CDs); 2004

SYMPHONIES, CONCERTS AND DOCUMENTARIES

Beethoven, Ninth Symphony
Nylund, Vermillion, Kaufmann, Selig, Gächinger Kantorei,
RSO Stuttgart, Norrington; Hänssler (CD); 2002 (live)

Schoenberg, *Die Jakobsleiter* and *Friede auf Erden*
Henschel, Kaufmann, Rügamer, Volle, Johnson, Azesberger,
Kammer, Heidi Meier and others, Deutsches Sinfonie-
Orchester Berlin, Nagano; harmonia mundi (CD); 2003

An Evening with Puccini
Arias and scenes from *Le villi*, *Edgar*, *Manon Lescaut*, *Tosca*,
Madama Butterfly, *La fanciulla del West*, *Suor Angelica*,
Turandot; Kaufmann, Filarmonica della Scala, Rieder; video
director: Large; Sony (DVD/Blu-ray); 2015 (live)

Verdi, *Requiem*
Harteros, Garanča, Kaufmann, Pape, Chorus and Orchestra of
La Scala, Milan, Barenboim; Decca (CD and DVD/Blu-ray);
2012

Wagner, Bicentenary Concert
Kaufmann, Dresden Staatskapelle, Thielemann; C Major
(DVD/Blu-ray); 2013

Opera Gala Live from Baden-Baden
Arias and orchestral excerpts by Wagner, Gounod, Mascagni,
Puccini, Boito and others; Harteros, Gubanova, Kaufmann,
Terfel, Badische Staatskapelle, Armiliato; Sony (DVD); 2017

Du bist die Welt für mich / Berlin 1930 (live concert and television documentary)
Songs and arias from operettas by Lehár, Kálmán, Tauber, Benatzky, Abraham and Künneke; cinema hits by Stolz, May, Heymann and Spoliansky; 'Glück, das mir verblieb' from Korngold's *Die tote Stadt*; Kaufmann, Kleiter, Berlin Radio Symphony Orchestra, Rieder; Sony (DVD/Blu-ray); 2014

Notes on the contributors

Nikolaus Bachler trained at the Max Reinhardt School in Vienna and spent many years working as an actor before becoming artistic director of the State Theatres in Berlin. From 1996 to 1999 he ran the Vienna Volksoper and from 1999 to 2009 was in charge of the city's Burgtheater. Since 2009 he has been the general manager of the Bavarian State Opera in Munich. The Burgtheater made him an honorary member in 2009.

Plácido Domingo is one of the most successful and versatile opera singers of our age with a repertory of some 140 roles. He made his professional stage debut in Mexico City in 1959 and by the middle of the following decade was launched on his international career. *The Three Tenors* concert at the World Championships in Rome in 1990 turned him into one of the megastars of today's music scene. Not only is he tirelessly active as a singer but also as a conductor, opera administrator and the founder of Operalia, an international competition for young singers.

Natalie Dessay won several international singing competitions before embarking on a career that has taken her all over the world in a repertory that includes not only the bel canto roles of Lucia and Amina (*La sonnambula*) but also the French repertory, notably Manon, Ophélie and Mélisande, as well as Richard Strauss's coloratura roles of Zerbinetta and Aminta (*Die schweigsame Frau*). Her Met performances of *Lucia di Lammermoor* and *La fille du régiment* were relayed to cinemas all over the world.

Helmut Deutsch continues to pursue an international career as a lieder accompanist, working with many of the world's leading recitalists. From 1967 to 1979 he taught at the Vienna College of Music and from 1986 to 2011 held a chair in lieder singing at the College of Music and Theatre in Munich. A visiting professor at the music colleges in Munich, Frankfurt and Nuremberg, he continues to give masterclasses throughout the whole of Europe.

Anja Harteros studied singing with Liselotte Hammes at Cologne's College of Music. After early engagements in Gelsenkirchen, Wuppertal and Bonn, she made her international breakthrough when she won the 1999 Cardiff Singer of the World Competition. Now one of the most sought-after singers in the world, she has enjoyed particular acclaim as Elsa (*Lohengrin*), Violetta (*La traviata*), Elisabetta (*Don Carlo*), Leonora (*La forza del destino*), Maddalena (*Andrea Chénier*) and the Marschallin (*Der Rosenkavalier*).

Jürgen Kesting was for many years arts editor on *stern* magazine, while also making a name for himself as a radio broadcaster and as the author of several books, including one on Maria Callas. His four-volume study *The Great Singers* is widely regarded as one of the most important publications in the field of singing. A revised edition appeared in 2008.

Christa Ludwig grew up in a household of singers and actors and was seventeen when she made her professional stage debut in Gießen. She was for many years a member of the ensemble of the Vienna State Opera, while simultaneously pursuing an international career as one of the leading German mezzo-sopranos of her generation, setting standards in opera and lieder recordings that have rarely been equalled. She retired from the stage in 1994 after a career lasting almost fifty years. Much sought after as a teacher, she also sits on the jury at international singing competitions.

Antonio Pappano was twenty-one when he began his career as a répétiteur at the New York City Opera. By the age of twenty-eight, he had already made his conducting debut with Den Norske Opera in Oslo. He became music director of the Brussels Opera in 1992 and was appointed to a similar position at Covent Garden in 1999 with effect from the 2002–3 season. Now widely regarded as one of the few genuine theatre conductors of our age, he was knighted in 2012.

Alexander Pereira was the general manager of the Zurich Opera from 1991 to 2012, during which time he consolidated the company's international reputation by building up a permanent ensemble of singers and staging a number of widely acclaimed new productions. From 2012 to 2014 he was the general manager of the Salzburg Festival. Since 2014 he has run La Scala, Milan.

Thomas Voigt is a freelance writer, journalist, film-maker and vocal coach. From 1992 to 1996 he edited *Opernwelt* and from 1998 to 2003 was editor-in-chief of *Fono Forum*. He has published biographies of Martha Mödl, Inge Borkh and Edda Moser and made documentary films about Fritz Wunderlich, Lisa Della Casa, Elisabeth Schwarzkopf, Robert Stolz and Jonas Kaufmann. For his services to journalism he was awarded the Gottlob Frick Medal in Gold.

Index of names